POCKET
LISBON

Sandra Henriques

Top: Santos (p130)
Bottom: Alfama (p66)

Contents

Plan Your Trip 4

FROM "TOP", KERRY MURRAY/LONELY PLANET © KERRY MURRAY/LONELY PLANET ©

★ Top Experiences

The Journey Begins Here

The appeal of Lisbon, bathed by the Atlantic at the western edge of Europe, is no secret. Thousands of travellers arrive every year – sometimes to the dismay of *lisboetas* (Lisbon residents) still not used to the crowds. They come to experience the city's best side: sunsets that turn Rio Tejo into liquid gold, food infused with herbs and olive oil, and cobblestone streets snaking uphill to *miradouros* (viewpoints) through tight clusters of buildings covered in *azulejos* (painted glazed tiles). I've seen many versions of Lisbon in my 30 years living here, some fondly missed, but the city has finally achieved its European capital status.

Sandra Henriques
@sandra.henriques.writer
Sandra is a published author of travel guides and horror books. Born in the Azores, she lived in the archipelago until moving to Lisbon in 1997.

Arco da Rua Augusta (p61)
KERRY MURRAY/LONELY PLANET ©

THE BEST

Nightlife Experiences

Lisbon's nightlife scene seems to have endless options: enjoying casual drinks at cultural bars with breaks for in-house films and DJ sets, clubbing until the break of dawn, and applauding performances by local artists.

Attend a pre-dinner live fado music show at unusual locations, such as **Pavilhão Chinês** (pictured). (p46)

Browse books, attend a concert and warm up for the night ahead with a DJ set at the cultural hub and bar **Casa do Comum**. (p44)

Bring out your best moves at one of the lip-sync jukebox events at **Drama Bar**, complete with glam accessories. (p81)

Dance to DJ sets or a live indie show or save your energy for dark-to-dawn clubbing at **Musicbox**. (p44)

Party until dawn and see one of the city's best drag shows at **Trumps**, Lisbon's most popular LGBTIQ+ nightclub. (p50)

Buy tickets for one of the monthly programs at **Cinema Nimas** and see classic independent films on the big screen. (p122)

Right: Alfama (p66)

THE BEST

Museum Experiences

Get under the skin of Portuguese art and history at museums tracing the country's recent past, small gallery-like places dedicated to Lisbon-born artists, cultural institutions with impressive collections and large-scale installations that address challenging topics.

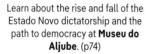

Learn about the rise and fall of the Estado Novo dictatorship and the path to democracy at **Museu do Aljube**. (p74)

Stroll through the four floors of **Museu Nacional de Arte Antiga**, admiring masterpieces from the 15th to the 19th centuries (pictured). (p128)

Discover design pieces across eight floors at **MUDE**, where the building itself is noteworthy. (p59)

Immerse yourself in the work of the namesake artists at **Fundação Arpad Szenes-Vieira da Silva**, a museum inside an old silk factory. (p120)

Admire Portugal's most extensive contemporary art collection at **Centro de Arte Moderna**. (p114)

See what contemporary issues artists address at the often-interactive art installations and temporary exhibitions at **MAAT Gallery** (pictured above and right). (p93)

Maat Central (p93)

THE BEST

Industrial Heritage Experiences

With factories turned into art museums and shopping centres, a bridge's pillar made into a viewpoint, grimy iron and shiny *azulejos* (painted glazed tiles), Lisbon's industrial heritage attractions show off this inventive city.

Learn about Ponte 25 de Abril and take in views from the bridge's seventh pillar at **Experiência Pilar 7**. (p136)

Shop and see street art at **LX Factory**, a commercial and creative hub inside an old thread factory. (p136)

Spot the early-20th-century housing blocks and quarters built for migrant factory workers and their families at **Vila Berta** in Graça. (p77)

Head to **MAAT Central** to see contemporary art shows and permanent exhibitions explaining how the former electricity plant powered Lisbon. (p93)

Take a shortcut from Chiado to Baixa on Lisbon's most famous lift, the early 1900s cast-iron, art nouveau **Elevador de Santa Justa**. (p63)

THE BEST

Food & Drink Experiences

Even the simplest fish grilled on hot coals drizzled with golden olive oil tastes heavenly and inspires Michelin-starred chefs to put their twist on traditional recipes. Enjoy classic and contemporary Portuguese cuisine and never skip dessert.

Toast the city with *ginjinha* (cherry liqueur) at **Ginjinha Sem Rival**, a local favourite bar in Baixa. (p62)

Sweeten your day with custard tarts at **Pastéis de Belém**. (p93)

Join locals for a simple dinner of grilled sardines on bread with salad, boiled potatoes and roasted peppers at **santos populares**. (p75)

Grab a seat at one of the canteen-style tables at **Mercado da Ribeira** and have lunch from a Portuguese chef's food stall. (p45)

Have coffee and a *bolo de arroz* (Portuguese rice muffin) at historic **Confeitaria Nacional** while admiring the cafe's original 19th-century decor. (p60)

Confeitaria Nacional (p60)

MAURO RODRIGUES/SHUTTERSTOCK ©

THE BEST

Modern Art Experiences

Home to unusual art galleries, free-to-visit street art, contemporary architecture designed by some of the best, and modernist projects that left a mark, Lisbon has art for everyone, from connoisseurs to casual viewers.

Check out the tile panels designed by visionary artist Maria Keil at some of the Lisbon Metro stations along the Blue and Yellow Lines, such as **São Sebastião**. (p119)

Descend into **WC**, Lisbon's most unusual art gallery, to see exhibitions by contemporary artists, designers and illustrators. (p118)

Take a walking tour through iconic examples of contemporary architecture and urban art in **Parque das Nações**. (p96)

See the latest street-art pieces at free-for-all **Galeria de Arte Urbana** (pictured left) while travelling in Elevador da Glória. (p46)

Step inside **Igreja de Nossa Senhora do Rosário de Fátima** (pictured above) to see Portuguese modernism masterpieces, stained-glass windows and mosaics by Almada Negreiros. (p119)

Right: Cat sculpture, Parque das Nações

THE BEST

History Experiences

The Romans named it Olisipo, the Visigoths knew it as Ulishbon and the Moors called it Al Ushbuna. Lisbon has many layers, most buried under the rubble of the 1755 earthquake. Some endured to tell the city's story.

See relics and the unearthed remains of an ancient Roman theatre at **Museu do Teatro Romano** (pictured). (p74)

Walk along the aisle of **Convento do Carmo**'s roofless Gothic church, one of the few structures that survived the 1755 earthquake. (p38)

Step inside 12th-century **Sé de Lisboa**, Lisbon's first Catholic church, built on top of a former mosque. (p74)

Admire every Manueline architectural detail of **Mosteiro dos Jerónimos**, the style's greatest symbol. (p86)

Pay tribute to prominent figures at **Panteão Nacional** (pictured), a church entangled in politics and scandals that took four centuries to complete. (p78)

Book a free tour of **Núcleo Arqueológico da Rua dos Correeiros** and discover more than 2000 years of history under a bank. (p55)

Right: Convento do Carmo (p38)

THE BEST

Outdoors Experiences

The sun shines practically all year, and *lisboetas* (Lisbon residents) make the best of good weather, even in winter. Urban parks with picnic tables, barefoot experiences at botanical gardens, riverside walks and romantic gardens: Lisbon has it all.

Pack a book and a blanket and head to Fundação Calouste Gulbenkian for a quiet break at **Jardim Gulbenkian** (pictured). (p115)

Feel the breeze and discover the east side walking route of **Parque Ribeirinho do Oriente**, which runs from Jardim do Neptuno in Parque das Nações to Marvila. (p105)

Find shelter from noisy traffic and feel leaves crunching under your bare feet in the sensory garden at **Jardim Botânico de Lisboa**. (p121)

Plan a picnic with the kids at Lisbon's lesser-known urban park **Tapada das Necessidades** (pictured) in Alcântara. (p135)

Stroll around the romantic and dog-friendly 19th-century **Jardim da Estrela** or sit with a drink at the lakeside cafe. (p132)

Head to the outdoor amphitheatre at **Jardim Amália Rodrigues** and admire the view of Avenida da Liberdade. (p119)

Best for Kids

Let little ones press their noses against the glass of the central tank at **Oceanário de Lisboa** (p99) as schools of carefree fish and other marine creatures swim by.

Take youngsters to **Centro de Ciência Viva** (p104) to blow off steam while learning with age-appropriate science-based activities and experiences.

Feel the earth shake under your feet in a controlled and safe environment at **Quake** (p91), a good spot for tweens with plenty of selfie stops.

Seek shelter from the rain or heat at small and cosy **Museu da Marioneta** (p134) to see puppets created by local and international artists.

Learn about Lisbon's public transit history, ride in a historic tram, and see a warehouse full of old buses and trams at **Museu da Carris** (p133).

Best for Free

See art exhibitions and occasional live music concerts for small audiences at **WC** (p118), an unexpected cultural venue in a former underground public restroom.

Browse for bargains, relics, vintage clothes, arts and crafts, and everything in between at **Feira da Ladra** (p76), Lisbon's oldest flea market happening twice a week in Alfama.

Attend concerts, live performances and family-friendly art workshops at **Jardins do Bombarda** (p118), the refurbished gardens of a former mental-health hospital, now run by community-based project Largo Residências.

Walk around Roman ruins and pieces of the city's old medieval wall on the ground floor of Renaissance building **Casa dos Bicos** (p78).

Stroll around Graça and spot early 1900s housing blocks and apartment buildings for migrant factory workers and their families, such as **Vila Berta** (p77).

Three Perfect Days

Hit Lisbon's biggest sights in the morning and then explore the city on foot in the afternoon. In the evening, explore nightlife hot spots or head to a local festival.

Castelo de São Jorge (p70)

━━━━ DAY ONE ━━━━

Only Have One Day?

MORNING

Head to 12th-century **Castelo de São Jorge** (p70) to take in the views over Lisbon and then walk down to **Miradouro de Santa Luzia** (p75) via the Roman ruins outside **Museu do Teatro Romano** (p74).

AFTERNOON

Stroll through the maze of narrow cobblestone streets in the heart of the historic centre to absorb the energy of **Alfama** (p67). Stop for a traditional Portuguese lunch at family-owned **Sardinha** (p79).

EVENING

Check out the Roman ruins inside **Casa dos Bicos** (p78; pictured) and then hop on bus 10B to **Largo da Graça** (p73). Finish the day with a concert, a cold beer and *petiscos* (food to share) at **Damas** (p81).

FROM LEFT: SILKY/SHUTTERSTOCK ©, MTCURADO/GETTY IMAGES ©, PELLE ZOLTAN/SHUTTERSTOCK ©, KYRYLO NEIEZHMAKOV/SHUTTERSTOCK ©

━━━ DAY TWO ━━━ ━━━ DAY THREE ━━━

A Weekend Trip

MORNING

Start the day off right with freshly baked custard tarts at **Pastéis de Belém** (p93; pictured). Spend the morning exploring **Mosteiro dos Jerónimos** (p86) and **Torre de Belém** (p85). Squeeze in a visit to **MAAT Gallery** (p93) before heading to the city centre.

AFTERNOON

Catch the train to Cais do Sodré for a late lunch at **Mercado da Ribeira** (p45), which Time Out transformed into a gourmet food court. Walk to Praça do Comércio and visit **Lisboa Story Centre** (p58) to learn about the city's history.

EVENING

Grab dinner at **Palácio Chiado** (p48) and head to Bairro Alto for drinks and dancing at **Casa do Comum** (p44).

A Short Break

MORNING

Take a scenic ride on tram 25E from Praça da Figueira to Campo de Ourique (Prazeres). Step inside **Cemitério dos Prazeres** (p134) to see the views and then explore the neighbourhood's shops and streets.

AFTERNOON

Take tram 25E to Estrela to visit **Basílica da Estrela** (p132; pictured). Cross the street to relax at romantic **Jardim da Estrela** (p132) and grab a quick lunch at one of the garden's kiosks.

EVENING

Walk 1km or take bus 713 to Santos. Wrap up the day with a charcuterie board paired with Portuguese wine at **Comida Independente** (p137).

If You Have More Time

Head to the east side to explore underwater marvels at **Oceanário de Lisboa** (p99) and see Parque das Nações from above while riding the cable car **Telecabine Lisboa** (p105).

Check what movies are on at independent film festivals at **Cinema São Jorge** (p122) and the monthly curated programmes at **Cinema Nimas** and **Cinemateca Portuguesa** (p122). Visit one of Lisbon's many art museums to discover the work of local creators. Top picks include **Fundação Arpàd Szenes–Vieira da Silva** (p120) and **Atelier-Museu Júlio Pomar** (p42).

Explore the lesser-known religious sites of **Convento dos Cardaes** (p47), **Igreja da Conceição Velha** (p61) and **Capela de Santo Amaro** (p135). Relax in nature at local favourites **Jardim Gulbenkian** (p115), **Tapada das Necessidades** (p135) or **Jardim Botânico de Lisboa** (p121).

Dance to the crack of dawn at **Musicbox** (p44) or have a quieter evening with a glass of Portuguese wine at **Entretanto Rooftop Bar** (p49).

Oceanário de Lisboa (p99)

GREG ELMS/LONELY PLANET ©

A City Day Trip

Catch an early train from Restauradores and spend the day in **Sintra** (p138). Start by visiting the two palaces with set designer Luigi Manini's unique style that blends Gothic and Renaissance architecture: **Quinta da Regaleira** (pictured) and **Palácio Biester**.

Head back to the historic centre for a pit stop at **Casa Piriquita** to try a classic *travesseiro,* the pillow-shaped puff pastry with egg cream and almond filling created at this cafe and pastry shop.

Before taking an evening train back to Lisbon, catch bus 434 to hit the hilltop main sites: **Palácio Nacional da Pena** and **Castelo dos Mouros**.

On a Rainy Day

You can easily spend a morning indoors browsing contemporary art at **Centro de Arte Moderna** (p114), 17th-century masterpieces at **Museu Nacional de Arte Antiga** (p128; pictured) or Portuguese design pieces at **Museu do Design** (p59).

Museu do Aljube (p74) and **Lisboa Story Centre** (p58) are great inside options for learning about local history.

If you're visiting Lisbon with kids, entertain them with science-inspired activities at **Centro de Ciência Viva** (p104) and **Museu Nacional de História Natural** (p122), and the puppet exhibitions at cosy **Museu da Marioneta** (p134). Those travelling with tweens should visit the more high-adrenaline, educational earthquake simulation experience at **Quake** (p91).

21

Get Prepared

Manners Matter

Keep to the right on escalators and moving walkways. Walk in single file on narrow pavements and avoid stopping abruptly for photos.

Most locals speak English but appreciate it if you start a conversation with *olá* (hello) or *desculpe* (excuse me). Don't take it to heart if you try speaking in Portuguese and *lisboetas* (Lisbon residents) reply in English. Some Portuguese words are hard to understand, so it's faster and easier that way.

Cultural Sensitivity

When going out for food and drinks, avoid boasting about how everything is cheap, no matter how much you think that remark is harmless. Some *lisboetas* struggle to make ends meet because local wages don't keep up with inflation, and they can't afford the cafes and restaurants they used to go to since those businesses increased their prices.

Things to Know

Coffee If you hang around long enough at a cafe, you'll hear a range of requests for a *bica* (espresso). If you're not particular about size, ask for *um café*. Order *italiana* if you want a short espresso, *curto* for a half-full cup and *cheio* for full to the brim. Local cafes don't serve coffee-based drinks beyond cappuccino, *galão* (a quarter coffee and three-quarters milk), *meia de leite* (half coffee and half milk in a large cup) and *abatanado* (similar to an Americano).

Olive oil Don't be afraid to soak fish in a pool of olive oil, but salads and potatoes are better with just a drizzle.

Pickpockets Be alert riding historic trams, especially 28E. The earlier in the day and the larger the crowd, the better for their 'business'.

TIPPING

Tipping isn't mandatory, but giving something extra for exceptional service is a common courtesy. Leave spare coins on the table at the restaurant or let them know you don't need change by saying *'fica assim'*.

Restaurants
For good service

Cafes & bars
For good service

Taxis
Round up to the next euro

Guided tours
For exceptional service

DAILY BUDGET

Budget: Less than €60

- Dorm bed in a hostel: from €30
- *Menu do dia* (all-inclusive lunch menu): under €15
- Museum tickets: €2-10
- 24-hour public transit ticket: €6.80

Midrange: €60-150

- Double room at a three-star hotel: from €100
- Brunch: from €15
- Guided walking tour (small groups): from €40
- Dinner at a *casa de fado*: from €50

Top End: More than €150

- Double room at a boutique hotel: from €200
- Dinner at a Michelin-starred restaurant: from €190
- Private guided tour: from €150

Currency
Euro (€)

Language
Portuguese

Time zone
Western European Time (GMT/UTC)

TIP

When using Google Maps or similar mobile apps, pay more attention to the elevation than the distance or time between places. Some walks appear easy, but the shortest itinerary might include steep hills and flights of stairs.

When To Go

Lisbon is sunny 300 days a year. Even in colder months when days are shorter, the weather is pleasant enough to sit at a cafe's *esplanada* (open-air terrace).

Spring swings between rainy days and weather that's warm enough for picnics and light sunbathing. The summer season brings school holidays and morning-to-evening beach days. Longer days mean visitors can do and see more, even if half the world decided to travel to Lisbon.

In autumn, with the peak of back-to-school season, the city is busier and traffic more chaotic; make the most of the weekdays to visit semi-deserted museums. Christmas festivities (December/January) take over most of the winter, filling the city with holiday cheer and season's sweets.

The Main Events

April: On 25 April, a multigenerational crowd marches down Avenida da Liberdade from Marquês de Pombal to Rossio, wielding red carnations to celebrate the anniversary of the **1974 revolution for democracy**.

June: People gather at *arraiais* (street festivals) throughout the month to celebrate **santos populares** (popular saints). The night of 12 June is the busiest. The historic centre attracts a large crowd, but the party spreads to every corner of Lisbon. Every *lisboeta* (Lisbon resident) has a strong opinion about which *arraial* is best.

May/June: All roads lead to Parque Eduardo VII for **Feira do Livro de Lisboa**. The often-packed annual book fair includes book launches and signings, live music, discussion panels and crowd-elbowing for an hour before closing when selected books have big discounts.

Lisbon

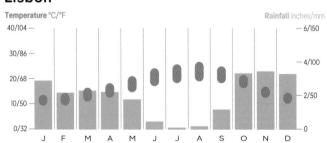

ECKHARD SUCHOWITZKY MEJIA/SHUTTERSTOCK ©

Santos populares celebration, Graça (p75)

June/July: Every other year, **Rock in Rio Lisboa** kicks off music festival season and transforms Parque Tejo into Cidade do Rock (Rock City) over two weekends. The lineup includes national and inter-national artists and established musicians.

Art, Film & Music Festivals

May/June: FIMFA takes national and international puppet theatre shows to several venues around Lisbon, ranging from adult-only performances to free plays for kids and families.

May: Multivenue **IndieLisboa** screens fresh and classic independent films, promotes industry workshops and talks, and hosts concerts (IndieByNight) and special sessions for kids (IndieJúnior).

August: Contemporary jazz concerts take over several spaces indoors and out at Fundação Calouste Gulbenkian during the month-long summer festival **Jazz em Agosto**.

September: The best new and cult-classic horror films fill the screens at Cinema São Jorge during the week-long **MOTELX**. Professional filmmakers compete for the coveted Best Portuguese Horror Short award.

ACCOMMODATION LOWDOWN

June to August are the most expensive months for accommodation. Baixa and the historic centre have the highest concentration of hotels and short-stay apartments. Before you book a bargain stay, check if the accommodation is easy to reach and if you have to haul luggage up steep streets or outdoor staircases.

✈ Getting There

Most visitors arrive in Lisbon by air, flying into Aeroporto Humberto Delgado (LIS). It's also possible to arrive by long-distance bus, cruise ship or international train.

From the Airport to the City Centre

By Ride Share or Taxi

Using a ride-share service (Uber or Bolt) is the most convenient way to travel from the airport. The compulsory pickup point is at the Kiss & Fly car park outside Departures. By law, all cars are identified with a TVDE sticker on the windshield's top right corner and another on the back window.

Standard taxis are also an easy way to get to the city. Pay in cash and budget for €15 to €20 (including luggage fees). A ride to the city centre takes about 30 minutes.

By Metro

Lisbon Metro's Red Line is the most affordable way to get to the city centre, and the ride takes about 20 minutes to São Sebastião. With only four lines, the Lisbon Metro network is easy to navigate.

Skip the long queues at the ticket offices and ticket machines at the airport by tapping your contactless debit or credit card at the validation gate. A one-way ticket costs €1.80.

By Bus

The Aerobus service ended in 2020, but there is still one option from the airport: bus 744, which ends in Restauradores. The trip costs €2.10 and can take up to one hour. Buses have limited space for luggage.

Other Points of Entry

Terminal de Cruzeiros de Lisboa

Most overseas ferries dock near Alfama. The terminal is served by various bus routes and is within walking distance of two Blue Line metro stations (Terreiro do Paço and Santa Apolónia).

Sete Rios

This international railway station has direct connections to Lisbon Metro's Blue Line (Jardim Zoológico), and the urban train to Entrecampos (served by the metro's Yellow Line) and Roma-Areeiro (Green Line).

Getting Around

Lisbon has a good public transportation network, including a metro, buses, trams and funiculars. Use urban Comboios de Portugal (CP) trains to skip traffic and reach further-away areas like Oriente and Belém. Reaching Trafaria on the south bank is faster by ferry. Opt for rideshares for cross-city trips or after 1am when transit options decrease.

Metro

The Lisbon Metro is the fastest and cheapest option to get around. The Blue Line covers Baixa, the Yellow Line goes to Marquês de Pombal and beyond, and the Green Line connects Cais do Sodré to Campo Grande via several stops within Mouraria. The Red Line intersects with the other three and is the best way to reach Parque das Nações and the airport. However, the metro's schedule (6.30am to 1am) limits nighttime travel. New stations are set to open in Santos and Estrela in 2025 and Alcântara by 2026.

Train

During rush hour, catching a CP urban train from Cais do Sodré to Belém (Cascais Line) and from Santa Apolónia to Oriente (Azambuja Line)

is a great way to avoid traffic and a better alternative to buses and trams.

Rideshares

Public transport options are fewer after 1am, and rideshares are the best option for getting around. You can opt for this alternative to cover

FROM LEFT: CHRISDORNEY/SHUTTERSTOCK ©, FOTOKON/SHUTTERSTOCK ©

─────── **ESSENTIAL APP** ───────
Download the official **Carris app** (carris.pt/en/travel/useful-information/it-applications) for trip planning and bus and tram schedules.

longer distances within the city to areas not served by metro or train.

Walking

Walking is the best way to get under the skin of Lisbon, particularly in the historic centre, but hills and slippery cobblestones when it rains might hinder the experience.

Trams & Funiculars

For many Lisbon commuters, trams are the only option to get to and from work, and they include highly touristic routes like 28E and 15E. Opt to ride these outside of rush hour or if no other options are available. To tackle the hills and shorten distances, use the funiculars: Bica (Cais do Sodré to Chiado), Glória (Rossio to Bairro Alto) and Graça (Mouraria to Graça). Because they are often mistaken for tourist rides (and 'sold' as such), expect long queues at any time of day.

E-Bikes

In Lisbon, installing proper bike lanes is a fad that fluctuates depending on who's in charge of the city council. The areas by the river (Santa Apolónia to Belém) and uptown from Marquês de Pombal to Campo Grande are the best places to get around on two wheels. Download **Gira** (gira-bicicletasdelisboa. pt), Lisbon's bike-sharing app, and ride for up to 45 minutes for €2.

Public Transport Essentials

Fares & Tickets

If you plan on using several public transport options in Lisbon, purchase the **Navegante card** (€0.50) at ticket machines and ticket offices in Lisbon Metro and train stations and top it up with pay-as-you-go credit (called Zapping). The card can be used to travel on buses, trams and funiculars (Carris); urban trains (CP and Fertagus); Lisbon Metro; and ferries (Transtejo). Navegante cards are valid for one passenger only.

Cards can be topped up with as much as €40, but unused credit can't be refunded. The pay-as-you-go option is cheaper than buying single tickets for each metro, bus and ferry trip. Account for a daily budget of €10 for round trips on the bus and metro.

Metro Tap & Go

If you plan to take the metro only, use your contactless debit or credit card to tap and go through the validation gates. One ride costs €1.80, and you can confirm the amount debited when tapping the card.

One-Day Tickets

One-day tickets are valid for 24 hours after the first validation. Load this prepaid ticket on a Navegante card (€0.50) at ticket machines and ticket offices at metro and train stations if you plan to travel extensively on Carris buses and the metro for one day. It costs €6.80.

Validating Tickets

You must validate your ticket on every public transit trip. Keep your purchase receipt in case the validator malfunctions.

Passengers must validate their tickets to enter and exit the metro platforms and most train stations. At ferry stations, you validate to enter the boarding waiting area. On buses, validation points are near the entrance at the front of the vehicle. On older trams, tickets are validated at the entrance at the front of the tram. Newer vehicles with more than one entrance usually have a second validation machine in the middle.

TRAVEL COSTS

On-board tram fare
€3.10

Zapping bus and metro fare
€1.61

Minimum adult train fare
€1.45

PUBLIC TRANSIT ETIQUETTE

Queue for buses, trams and funiculars. Let people off the metro and trains before entering.

TICKETS

Transport	Regular fare	Zapping
Urban trains	from €1.45	€2 (all zones)
Ferry to Trafaria	€1.45	€1.40
Funiculars (Bica, Glória, Lavra)	€4.10	€4.10
Bus and metro	€1.80	€1.61

TRAIN TICKET ZONES

1

Within Lisbon and trips between Belém and Algés.

2/3

From Lisbon to suburban areas in Oeiras, Cascais, Amadora and Loures.

4

Trips from Cais do Sodré to Cascais, and Rossio to Sintra.

🎁 A Few Surprises

Find art old and new in unusual locations, and traces of Lisbon's history scattered around the city, hidden in plain sight.

Art Underground

Thanks to modernist painter Maria Keil, who came up with the idea of decorating the metro's first stations with tile panels in 1959, every subway station in Lisbon features art. Keil's geometric patterns brighten up the lobby and platforms of nine stations on the Blue and Yellow Lines. The strong-coloured design of Olaias, a station on the Red Line, created by prominent Portuguese artists in 1998, is, perhaps, the most exuberant.

Pre-Earthquake Lisbon

In 1755, an earthquake caused most of Lisbon to be buried under rubble, and in the post-quake reconstruction, new buildings completely covered the old. Over time, with each building renovation or change in the city layout, pieces of history have started to see the light of day again: parts of Olisipo (the Roman Empire's name for Lisbon) in Alfama and Baixa; remains of the first city wall Cerca Velha (post-Roman period and pre-Christian invasions) in Castelo and Alfama when Lisbon was the Islamic city of Al Ushbuna; and sections of the 14th-century medieval wall Cerca Fernandina in Mouraria and Chiado.

Pavement QR Codes

Mind your step and look down to find QR codes that you can scan to get more information about local culture and important historical events in Lisbon. Look for them around Mouraria, Castelo and Alfama (about the history of fado); Bairro Alto and Chiado (tracing the events leading to the democratic revolution on 25 April 1974); and Baixa (pinpointing the sites of Roman Lisbon).

OFFBEAT LISBON

Descend into **WC** (p118), a repurposed public toilet, to see art exhibitions and attend intimate concerts.

Head to LGBTIQ-friendly **Drama Bar** (p81) in Graça for themed parties, drag shows and lip-sync jukebox events.

Find out all there is to know about salted cod at **Centro Interpretativo da História do Bacalhau** (p58).

Buy a ticket for **Real Fado** (p46) concerts, which take place in unusual venues across Príncipe Real.

NICHOLAS COURTNEY/SHUTTERSTOCK ©

Cerca Fernandina (p78)

AMNAT30/SHUTTERSTOCK ©

Live fado music, Alfama (p77)

Explore Lisbon

Parque das Nações (p96)
MAURO RODRIGUES/SHUTTERSTOCK ©

See p48
for eating,
drinking and
shopping
listings

Explore
Bairro Alto & Chiado

Bairro Alto and Chiado share part of the same high hill in Lisbon, but that's it when it comes to common ground. Bairro Alto is a medieval grid of narrow streets, where buildings are so close to one another that neighbours can peek through the window. Chiado has high-end boutiques and shops, small leafy squares *(largos),* historic theatres, and old *pastelarias* (pastry shops) and cafes. Bairro Alto is a quiet residential quarter by day and a noisy bar-hopping destination by night. Chiado bustles from breakfast until evening and then winds down. Praça Luís de Camões marks the border between the two.

Getting Around

 Walking

Walking is the best way to explore Bairro Alto and Chiado. Expect slippery cobblestones in the rainy season and mind the traffic in streets with narrow pavements.

 Funicular

Avoid the uphill walk to reach these neighbourhoods by jumping on one of the funiculars: Glória from Baixa or Bica from Cais do Sodré.

 Metro

The Blue and Green Lines intersect at Baixa-Chiado station, where you can experience Lisbon residents' oldest grudge: the broken escalators at the Largo do Chiado exit.

★

THE BEST

VIEWPOINT Miradouro de São Pedro de Alcântara (p46)

STREET ART Galeria de Arte Urbana (p46)

HISTORIC SITE Convento do Carmo (p38)

ALTERNATIVE AREA The Triangle (p42)

BAR Casa do Comum (p44)

Funicular, Bairro Alto
KERRY MURRAY/LONELY PLANET ©

1
2
3
4

Elevador da Lavra

2 Ascensor da Glória

Av da Liberdade

R da Glória

Cç da Glória

Pç dos Restauradores

Restauradores

Estação do Rossio

ROSSIO

R Áurea

22 Carmo Rooftop

Convento do Carmo & Museu Arqueológico **6**

Largo do Carmo

CHIADO

R da Condessa

R da Oliveira

57

Le Trindade Coelho

R da Misericórdia **45**

Galeria de Arte Urbana

23 Miradouro de São Pedro de Alcântara

26 Elevador da Glória

Elevador da Glória

R das Gáveas

Tv da Espera

R do Grémio Lusitano

Tv do Corpo

R da Água Flor

Tv da Boa Hora

Jardim dos Namorados

21

R das Talpas

R da Glória

R da Conceição da Glória

R Male d'Ávila

R Dom Pedro V

Casa do Comum

9

68

Pavilhão Chinês

18

30

31

Convento dos Cardaes

28

MOBA **27**

R da Atalaia

R da Rosa

R Luz Soriano

Zé dos Bois **10**

6

11

Tasca dos Canários Amarelos

BAIRRO ALTO

R do Século

Tv das Mercês

R das Flores de Deus

32

49

Cç do Combro

BAIRRO ALTO

R Academia Ciências

R Eduardo Coelho

R da Vinha

EmbaiXada **20**

Jardim Botânico

Real Fado **17**

Reservatório da Patriarcal **19**

Jardim do Príncipe Real

PRÍNCIPE REAL

R Cecílio de Sousa

R da Escola Politécnica

R de São Marçal

R da Palmeira

Pç das Flores

R de São Marça

R Nova da Piedade

Tv da Arrochela

R da Cruz dos Poiais

Atelier-Museu Júlio Pomar **1**

Tv Convento de Jesus

R Vale

Tv da Pereira

Tv da Palmeira

Cç Ene Miguel Pais

R da Monte do Carmo

R das Imprensa Nacional

A
B
C
D
E
F

36

Café A Brasileira

Livraria
Bertrand

Lg da Academia
Nacional de
Belas Artes

R Ivens
R Capelo
R Serpa Pinto
R dos Duques de Bragança
R Antônio Maria Cardoso
R do Alecrim

Pç do
Município

R do Arsenal
R Vítor Cordón

Av da Ribeira das Naus

Baixa-
Chiado

Musicbox

R Bernardino Costa

Quiosque
Ribeira das Naus

Lg do
Barão de
Quintela

R das Flores

R do Atáide
R da Emenda

CAIS DO
SORDÉ

Tv Carvalho

R dos Remolares

Mercado
da Ribeira

Cais do
Sodré

Discoteca
Jamaica

R da Cintura do Porto de Lisboa

R do Loreto
R da Horta Seca
R das Chagas
R do Sequeiro
R da Lapinha
Tv da Palmeira
Tv do Cabral

R da Ribeira Nova

Pç Dom
Luís I

Ascensor
da Bica

R Dom Luís I

Av 24 de Julho

Tokyo
Lisboa

Rio Tejo

SANTA
CATARINA

Tv da Alcáide
Tv de Santa Catarina
R Marechal Saldanha
R Fernandes Tomás

The Mill

Forninho
de São Roque

Dear
Breakfast

Hello, Kristof

R da Boavista

R do Instituto Industrial

C Marquês Abrantes

R de São Bento

R de São Bento

R Galvotas

For more see

⭐ Top Experiences p38
🎯 Experiences p42
🍴 Eating p48
🍷 Drinking p49
🛍 Shopping p51

400 m
0.25 miles

Convento do Carmo

One of the few notable buildings that partially survived Lisbon's Great Earthquake in 1755, the Gothic church at Convento do Carmo remains without a roof, and its high stone arches seem to reach for the sky.

MAP P36, **F4**

PLANNING TIP

Convento do Carmo is one of the most popular sites in the neighbourhood. For a quiet experience and to fully admire the convent's ruins, arrive at 10am when it opens.

Scan this QR code for opening hours and museum history.

In Ruins

It's said that the 14th-century church of **Convento do Carmo** (*museuarqueologicodocarmo.pt; adult/child €7/free*) remains in ruins to remind visitors of the devastation of the 1755 earthquake. This story sounds good in a brochure, but there's more to it. When Portugal dissolved the monasteries in 1834, renovations of the convent stopped indefinitely. It was perfect timing, as the Romantic artistic age was starting in Portugal, and ruins and old medieval monuments were the 19th-century movement's favourite aesthetic.

Historical context aside, walking down the central aisle under the arches of a roofless Gothic church is unique and, weather-permitting, it's where visitors spend most of their time.

Archaeological Museum

The admission ticket includes the archaeological museum at the back of the convent, and its collection of artefacts is small but wide ranging. Expect to spend about 30 minutes visiting **Museu Arqueológico do Carmo**. Space is tight, and it can be uncomfortable when it's crowded.

The medieval vaulted ceilings and stained-glass windows draw your eyes upward first before landing on the scattered baroque tile panels, tombstones and parts of Roman columns. Rooms 1 and 2 (which contain traces from pre-Portugal

CHRISDORNEY/SHUTTERSTOCK ©

civilisations), Room 3 (where Nuno Álvares Pereira, the convent's founder, is buried), and Room 4 (with an Egyptian sarcophagus and pre-Columbian artefacts) attract the most attention.

The video installation, in Portuguese and English, playing in the old sacristy gives a succinct account of the history. Skip it or take the opportunity to sit inside one of the convent's original sections before moving on.

Cultural Events

From video-mapping experiences to plays and concerts, Convento do Carmo puts on several outdoor cultural events in spring and summer, frequently with a version in English. Check the website for the latest events and information on how to buy tickets. The immersive video show 'Lisbon Under Stars' has been one of the most popular recurring events.

QUICK BREAK
Head to **Carmo Rooftop** (carmorooftop.pt) behind the convent for drinks or a meal. This casual cafe and bar has one of the best views in Lisbon.

🚶 WALKING TOUR

Walk Bairro Alto

By day, Bairro Alto is quiet, with just a handful of shops and restaurants open for business, and it feels almost deserted – very different from its nightly persona as a bar-hopping destination. Observe old buildings and neighbourhood life while strolling through the narrow streets of this 500-year-old quarter.

START	END	LENGTH
Jardim do Príncipe Real	Praça Luís de Camões	1.3km; 1 hour

1 Ancient Tree

In Bairro Alto's most famous garden, **Jardim do Príncipe Real**, notice the wide tree in the centre, resting its branches on a wrought-iron structure. This 150-year-old cypress is the oldest tree in Lisbon and continues to shelter many visitors in its shade.

2 Romantic Viewpoint

Walk down Rua Dom Pedro V through restaurants, shops and famous bars until you reach Lisbon's most romantic viewpoint: the two-terraced **Miradouro de São Pedro de Alcântara**. Take in the views over the Baixa neighbourhood, the surrounding hills, and tourists travelling in the Glória funicular up and down the steep cobblestone street.

3 Lottery Ticket Sellers' Square

Continue walking south (mind the traffic – the pavement is narrow) to a small square across from Igreja de São Roque. Largo Trindade Coelho is the official name, but everyone calls it **Largo do Cauteleiro** because of the statue honouring the old lottery ticket sellers. Some still sell lottery tickets in the streets, especially around Christmas and Easter.

4 Bar Neighbourhood

Cross the street to Travessa da Queimada to enter the heart of Bairro Alto's nightlife district. Known for

popular *casa de fado* (traditional restaurant where *fadistas* sing at regular intervals between courses at dinner) **Café Luso**, this side street has bars and restaurants that are a mix of new and trendy with the more established.

5 Historic Street

Take a slight detour to the right at Rua da Atalaia. Today, it's called Cheers Irish Pub Lisbon, but in the 1980s, not long after the democratic revolution, **Frágil** was one of the first bars in post-dictatorship Lisbon where everyone could feel genuinely free regardless of their professional status, sexual orientation or political affiliation.

6 Street Art

Continue south down Rua da Atalaia and turn left at Travessa dos Fiéis de Deus. Notice the António Alves and RIGO **street-art mural**, inspired by 1970s post-dictatorship working-class propaganda. The narrow street makes it a little hard to photograph it fully, but give it a shot.

7 'Let's Meet at Camões'

Turn right down Rua da Barroca, left on Rua das Salgadeiras and right at Rua do Norte. Across the street is **Praça Luís de Camões**, bustling with tourists and tour guides. Even with GPS and phone maps, many still arrange to meet at Camões before getting drinks in Bairro Alto.

EXPERIENCES

Admire Contemporary Art at Atelier-Museu Júlio Pomar

MUSEUM

MAP: **1** P36 **B4**

It's a two-for-one experience of contemporary art at **Atelier-Museu Júlio Pomar** *(ateliermu seujuliopomar.pt; adult/child €2/ free)*. First, it's an opportunity to step inside a building redesigned by award-winning Portuguese architect Siza Vieira, who transformed a former warehouse at the edge of Bairro Alto into a bright, open space over two floors. Second, it houses the art of Júlio Pomar, one of the most prominent artists in Portugal, who continuously learned from others and created new work until he died in 2018.

The building was imagined as the artist's workshop (Pomar lived across the street), but renovation took longer than anticipated. Instead, it became a museum with the heart of an atelier. Pomar displayed his work in a creative dialogue with newer artists' pieces that he discovered and selected, and the museum curators carry on the task, putting together new exhibitions every six months.

Explore The Triangle

AREA

An unofficial quarter is wedged between Bairro Alto and Cais do Sodré that local business owners dubbed 'The Triangle', a cluster of three streets (Poço dos Negros, Poiais de São Bento and São Bento)

that forms a perfect triangle on Lisbon's map.

When gentrification hit the historic centre in 2016, many independent businesses found a home at The Triangle, welcomed by older establishments that have been in the area for decades. While this part of Lisbon isn't completely immune to gentrification, most of it remains authentic, with speciality coffee shops and all-day breakfast spots, such as **The Mill** (MAP: **2** P36 **B5**; *themill.pt*), **Hello, Kristof** (MAP: **3** P36 **A5**; *hellokristof. com*) and **Dear Breakfast** (MAP: **4** P36 **A5**; *dearbreakfast.com*), next to traditional *pastelarias* – the cosy **Forninho de São Roque** (MAP: **5** P36 **A5**; *panifsroque.pt*) is one of my favourites. Convenience stores are steps away from gourmet food and drink retailers Mercearia Poço dos Negros and Companhia Portugueza do Chá (p51).

Take a Break at Largo do Carmo

SQUARE

MAP: **6** P36 **F4**

Largo do Carmo is Chiado's most picturesque square, with jacaranda trees lining the *calçada portuguesa* (Portuguese cobblestone pavement), queues to Convento do Carmo snaking around the 18th-century water fountain in the centre and the busy-all-year kiosk cafe in the corner.

Most Portuguese link Carmo to historic photos taken by Mário

Varela Gomes and Alfredo Cunha from 25 April 1974, which showed people perched on trees and lamp-posts and squeezed onto narrow balconies, eager to see the ongoing peaceful revolution. People had rushed to the square as news spread of the end of a five-decade-long dictatorship. The tiny square became a symbol of victorious democracy.

Browse Bertrand, the World's Oldest Bookstore BOOKS

MAP: **7** P36 **F5**

At first sight, the building covered in blue and white *azulejos* (painted glazed tiles), with a chipped wood-framed door and large windows showcasing books, is just another shop on Chiado's Rua Garrett. But a closer look at the corner showcase reveals the year that **Livraria Bertrand** (*bertrand.pt*) was founded (1732), which makes it the world's oldest operating bookstore, according to Guinness World Records.

Wooden cabinets filled with bestsellers and literary merchan-dise line the walls of the shop's seven rooms, which are named after Portuguese authors, some of whom roamed these same rooms almost 300 years ago. The shop has few windows, so the high ceilings compensate for the inevitable resort to artificial light.

The cafe in the back of the store is a sign that Bertrand has kept up with the times, when books are no longer enough to attract shoppers.

Join Pessoa for Coffee at Café A Brasileira CAFE

MAP: **8** P36 **E5**

Sculptor Lagoa Henriques' bronze statue of writer Fernando Pessoa (1888–1935) outside **Café A Brasileira** (*abrasileira.pt*) is a misinterpreted tourist attraction – the sculptor depicted the socially awkward poet waving people off, not inviting them to sit.

Portuguese modernism was born here thanks to Pessoa and three other regular customers and artists. A Brasileira's popular status means an often-crowded *esplanada* (open-air terrace),

 THE 1988 CHIADO FIRE

In the summer of 1988, a violent fire consumed Chiado's department stores to the dismay of tired firefighters trying to control the flames without fire engines, which weren't able to get closer to the location because of unmovable concrete flowerbeds in Rua do Carmo that obstructed emergency vehicles, as the teams found out at the scene. The fire rapidly spread and destroyed most of the neighbourhood's 18th-century buildings. Portuguese architect Siza Vieira led the reconstruction project, managing to restore the original facades of Armazéns do Chiado and the buildings at Rua Garrett and Rua do Carmo.

loud performances outside and a whirlwind of tourists seeking that perfect shot with the statue. Skip all that: it's the art nouveau facade, the art deco interior and the paintings hanging above the shelves behind the counter that are worthy of your attention. You can enjoy them all for the cost of an (admittedly overpriced) espresso (€2.50) at the counter or, if you're lucky, an empty table.

Bar Hop Through Bairro Alto   BAR

A peaceful residential neighbourhood by day, Bairro Alto transforms into a packed nighttime destination after midnight on weekends. Cup-holding crowds (a mix of tourists and locals) fill the narrow streets until bars close at 2am and then head to Cais do Sodré for clubbing.

Most Bairro Alto bars are too small to accommodate large numbers of customers, making people factor in the menu and prices rather than ambience when choosing where to go. Most end up on a pub crawl down one of the main streets (Rua da Atalaia, Rua da Barroca, Rua da Rosa and Rua do Diário de Notícias).

For the stick-to-one-place folks, try **Casa do Comum** (MAP: ❾ P36 C2; *casadocomum.org)*, a cultural spot with a bar, a Ler Devagar bookstore and a cinema; **Zé dos Bois** (MAP: ❿ P36 D4; *zedosbois. org)*, which offers live music by established and up-and-coming performers; or laid-back and affordable **Tasca dos Canários Amarelos** (MAP: ⓫ P36 D4; *facebook .com/TascaDosCanarios)*.

Dance at Clubs in Cais do Sodré   CLUB

In recent years, *lisboetas* (Lisbon residents) have witnessed the closing of historic nightclubs in Cais do Sodré because of real estate pressure to turn the old buildings housing these clubs into hotels and apartment blocks. The ones that remain have managed to dodge the trend – so far.

Musicbox (MAP: ⓬ P36 E7; *music boxlisboa.com)* has stood its ground as an eclectic cornerstone

'SILENCE, PLEASE'

In 2024, some areas in Bairro Alto (Rua da Atalaia), Chiado (Rua do Loreto, Praça Luís de Camões) and Cais do Sodré (Largo de São Paulo) got new signs with blue circles asking for bar-hoppers to be quiet. While the legal closing time for bars in these neighbourhoods is between 11pm and 2am, many push the limit and continue to sell drinks behind closed doors, serving patrons who gather outside. Partying crowds and cheap alcohol don't mix well with residential neighbourhoods, but this combination is decades old in Lisbon. What's changed? Most residents, some of them new, are finally at their wit's end.

of Cais do Sodré's music scene for almost two decades and has a packed calendar of concerts and DJ sets. After midnight, it's clubbing time. **Tokyo Lisboa** (MAP: ⑬ P36 **C8**; *instagram.com/tokyolisboa)* and **Discoteca Jamaica** (MAP: ⑭ P36 **D8**; *instagram.com/jamaica_lisboa)* are two other survivors that managed to stay open by moving away from the nightlife hub and closer to Rio Tejo. They remain classic hangouts for clubbers who enjoy dancing to indie and classic rock hits.

Eat Critic-Approved Dishes at Mercado da Ribeira
MARKET

MAP: ⑮ P36 **D7**

In 2014, public opinion diverged when **Mercado da Ribeira** was split in two. The fresh produce market remained in the east wing, and **Time Out Market** *(timeout market.com)*, a curated food court featuring the best of Lisbon, took the west wing. The concept was original, but *lisboetas* were distrustful of hipsters and gentrification rebranding everything old and authentic.

Though not all residents have made their peace with it a decade later, Time Out Market is the only place in Lisbon where you can taste Portuguese cuisine from more than 20 restaurants under one roof. Selected by the magazine's journalists, the places include classics like **Café de São Bento**

(unquestionably the best steak in Lisbon) and **Pinóquio** (seafood) and food from contemporary chefs Henrique Sá Pessoa and Susana Felicidade.

Lounge by the River in Cais do Sodré
WATERFRONT

MAP: ⑯ P36 **E8**

Sun-seeking visitors cover every free inch of staircases, street benches and walls on sunny mornings and afternoons between artist Almada Negreiros' sculpture *Reminiscência* to Cais do Gás. The terrace at **Quiosque Ribeira das Naus** *(instagram.com/ribeiradas nausquiosque)* is perhaps one of the most coveted places for chilling, especially if you're lucky enough to secure one of the lounge chairs.

Between Cais das Pombas and Cais do Sodré's ferry station, the converted warehouses accommodate a few family-friendly cafes and restaurants with smaller outdoor sitting areas.

Listen to Fado in Unusual Locations
LIVE MUSIC

On UNESCO's intangible heritage list since 2011, melancholic fado is the type of music that needs to be felt, not explained. Travellers looking for that unique experience gravitate to classic *casas de fado* or more casual *tascas* (taverns where your tab for wine and snacks includes an extra fee to pay for the performance).

But if you want the music only (drinks optional), try **Real Fado** (MAP: ⑰ P36 C1; *realfadoconcerts.com*). The one-hour concerts (7pm to 8pm) take place at unconventional locations in Príncipe Real: bar **Pavilhão Chinês** (MAP: ⑱P36 C2) on Thursday, underground reservoir **Reservatório da Patriarcal** (MAP: ⑲ P36 B2) on Friday and Saturday, and concept store and gallery **EmbaiXada** (MAP: ⑳ P36 C1; *embaixa dalx.pt*) on Sunday. Despite the unexpected stages, the same rules of etiquette apply – when the *fadista* sings, the audience must be silent.

Ride Historic Funiculars
FUNICULAR

Ascensor da Bica (MAP: ㉑ P36 C6) and **Ascensor da Glória** (MAP: ㉒ P36 E1; *carris.pt; return trip €4.10)* have helped *lisboetas* avoid the steep walk uphill from Cais do Sodré to Chiado and from Baixa to Bairro Alto since the early 1900s. Nowadays, with newer and faster alternatives, it's rare to spot locals amongst the tourists who don't mind waiting in line for the ride.

Bica's trip is a little smoother than Glória's, but both funiculars shamelessly shake their passengers no matter how hard the driver tries to lessen the distress. Fortunately, the journey ends (usually with a metal-on-metal screech) less than five minutes after departure. After exiting the car, get that postcard-perfect shot standing by the funicular.

Relax with a View at Miradouro de São Pedro de Alcântara
VIEWPOINT

Calling **Miradouro de São Pedro de Alcântara** (MAP: ㉓ P36 D2) a lookout doesn't do this two-tiered 18th-century garden justice. Think of it as a terrace leaning over the city. Grab a seat on one of the benches near the wrought-iron rail and admire Lisbon for as long as you like, while accepting it probably won't be in complete quiet because of its popularity.

Even if you stay for only a few minutes, check out the 1952 tile panel of Lisbon and compare it with what you see today. **Jardim dos Namorados** (MAP: ㉔ P36 D2) on the lower terrace is less popular but worth the detour in the daytime to take in the garden's romantic atmosphere of wrought-iron balconies and lampposts, baroque busts of Greek gods, and the carefully manicured lawns among cobblestone pavements.

Spot New Street Art at Galeria de Arte Urbana
PUBLIC ART

The brightly spray-painted walls at **Galeria de Arte Urbana** (MAP: ㉕ P36 D2; *gau.cm-lisboa.pt*) almost go unnoticed as tourists pay their undivided attention to **Elevador da Glória** (MAP: ㉖ P36 D3) screeching up and down the hill. Those travelling uphill in the funicular get a closer look at the seven panels lining the east side of Calçada da Glória. If you're exploring the neighbourhood on foot, to have a closer look at the street art pieces walk down from the funicular's stop next to Miradouro de São Pedro de Alcântara (with special care for slippery cobblestones on rainy days). In 2009, the Lisbon City Council's Department of Culture created these street-art galleries to dissuade graffiti artists from spraying monuments. Glória's walls remain open and free for street artists to use.

See Artisans at Work at MOBA

ARTS & CRAFTS

MAP: **27** P36 **D3**

Bairro Alto's former produce market now contains **MOBA** (Mercado de Ofícios do Bairro Alto), which is home to half a dozen artisans. Past the sliding door (if it's stuck, don't be afraid to push it) and to the right is **Latoaria Maciel** (*latoariamaciel.com*), a family-owned company that has specialised in tinwork since the 1800s. The company created many of the old light fixtures in Lisbon's streets and also produced work for Vermelho, fashion designer Christian Louboutin's hotel in Melides. Joining them are ceramist **Madre Deus** (*madredeusbs.com*) and furniture restorer Rita Boavida.

On weekdays from 9am to 6pm, the door is open to visitors and potential buyers.

Take a Tour of Convento dos Cardaes

CONVENT

MAP: **28** P36 **C2**

Tucked away on the border street between Bairro Alto and Príncipe Real, **Convento dos Cardaes** (*conventodoscardaes.com; adult/child €7/3*) is easy to miss, and many walk past it without realising that behind those plain walls is one of the few buildings that survived the 1755 earthquake.

Knowledgeable volunteers guide visits to this 17th-century convent, leading you around the baroque church (all original except the roof that collapsed) decorated with Dutch tile panels, marble floors and an impressive gold carved main altar. In the sacristy and beyond, a rich collection of religious art awaits, including rare and unusual pieces. With a much smaller community of nuns than when it was founded (1681), Convento dos Cardaes is still active, and its artisanal production of marmalades has a word-of-mouth level of fame. Grab a jar at the shop on your way out.

Best Places for...

Ⓔ Budget ⒺⒺ Midrange ⒺⒺⒺ Top End

See p36 for map of locations

Eating

Fusion

Palácio Chiado ⒺⒺ
㉙ E5

Art is all around in this remodelled, surprisingly laid-back 18th-century palace in Chiado, including on the plate where Portuguese classic dishes get international twists. *palaciochiado.pt; 12.30-4pm & 7pm-midnight Sun-Wed, to 2am Thu-Sat*

Tapisco ⒺⒺ
㉚ C2

Chef Henrique Sá Pessoa's menu fuses Spanish and Portuguese food to share at his restaurant whose name mixes tapa and *petisco* (snacks). *tapisco.pt; noon-4pm & 6.30pm-midnight Mon-Fri, noon-midnight Sat & Sun*

A Cevicheria ⒺⒺ
㉛ C2

Brazilian-Portuguese chef Kiko adds his multicultural upbringing to all his creations. At this Peruvian restaurant in Príncipe Real, the ceviche dishes have a Portuguese twist. *acevicheria.pt; noon-11pm*

Portuguese

Adega do Tagarro ⒺⒺ
㉜ C4

Typically loud and full, this Portuguese restaurant is a good stop for a meal before getting drinks in Bairro Alto. *instagram.com/adega _do_tagarro; noon-3pm & 7-11pm Mon-Sat*

Zapata ⒺⒺ
㉝ B5

Old-school restaurant that still tapes a handwritten menu on the wall. *noon-11pm Wed-Mon*

Tasca Zebras ⒺⒺ
㉞ C5

In a neighbourhood overrun by tourist-trap *tascas*, Zebras is a sight for sore eyes. This tiny place near Bica proudly serves simple, honest Portuguese food. *tasca zebras.com; noon-midnight Thu-Tue*

Taberna da Rua das Flores ⒺⒺ
㉟ D5

Everything is old school at this small *tasca* in Chiado, from the menu on slate tablets to the Portuguese dishes. *instagram .com/tabernadasflores; noon-11.30pm Mon-Sat, to 6pm Sun*

Casual Eats

Tricky's ⒺⒺ
㊱ B6

Contemporary dishes, including plant-based options, paired with signature cocktails and local and international wines. *cometotrickys.com; 7pm-midnight Tue-Sat*

Collect ⒺⒺ
㊲ D7

Perfect spot for a latenight burger and cocktail before or after browsing through the record store upstairs. *collect.pt; noon-1am*

Sol e Pesca Ⓔ
㊳ D7

Casual tapas that specialises in tinned fish, with a wide range of brands and types of preserves. *instagram.com/solepesca; noon-2am*

Vegetarian & Vegan

Jardim das Cerejas

39 F4

Small restaurant near Largo do Carmo serving affordable vegan buffets for lunch and dinner; children's menu available. *noon-3.30pm & 7-11pm Mon-Sat*

Organi Chiado

40 F5

Vegan restaurant in Chiado serving meals made with locally sourced ingredients. The menu changes daily and includes sugar- and dairy-free drinks. *organi.pt; noon-3.30pm & 7-11pm*

Ao 26

41 D5

Varied vegan menu, including plant-based versions of traditional local dishes and a good selection of Portuguese vegan wines. *instagram.com/26veganfoodproject; 12.30-6pm & 7-11pm*

A Colmeia

42 D5

At this cafeteria-style restaurant near Praça Luís de Camões, affordable menus include a main dish, a dessert or drink,

and salad. Cash only. *12.30-3pm Mon-Sat*

Cheap & Hearty Lunch

O Gaiteiro

43 C6

Tiny traditional restaurant next to Ascensor da Bica serving Portuguese-style meat and fish dishes in generous and affordable portions. *noon-4pm Tue-Sat*

O Trevo

44 E5

Home to Lisbon's best *bifana* (a marinated pork steak sandwich served grilled on crisp bread with mustard on the side), this corner restaurant is a busy mix of tourists and regulars. *instagram.com/otrevo48; 7am-10pm Mon-Sat*

Cafes

Pastelaria Benard

45 E5

This historic cafe started as a high-class teahouse in 1868. If you're overwhelmed by the pastry selection, the croissants served warm are a good bet. *benard.pt; 8.30am-11pm Mon-Sat*

Manteigaria

46 D5

With little room to drink coffee at the counter while savouring freshly baked *pastéis de nata*

(custard tarts), it's best to buy them to go. Each fresh batch is announced with bell-ringing. *facebook.com/manteigaria.oficial; 8am-midnight*

Pastelaria Emenda

47 D5

Traditional cafe perfect for a no-frills, typical Portuguese breakfast of a ham and cheese sandwich and *galão* (coffee and milk). *instagram.com/pastelariaemenda; 6.30am-7pm Mon-Fri, to 4pm Sat*

Drinking

Rooftop Bars

Entretanto Rooftop Bar

48 F5

Sip a glass of Portuguese wine at Hotel do Chiado's cosy restaurant and bar with a view of Castelo de São Jorge on the opposite hill. *hoteldochiado.pt; 11.30am-10pm*

Zé dos Bois

Known by locals as ZDB (p44), this art centre in the heart of Bairro Alto has a popular terrace bar. *zedosbois.org; 6pm-2am Tue-Sat*

Park
 C4

Rooftop bars weren't trending in Lisbon when this spot opened on the top floor of a car park. Hard to find, but the views are worth it. *facebook.com/parklisboaofficial; 4pm-2am Mon-Thu, from 2pm Fri & Sat*

Cocktails

A Tabacaria
 D6

Custom-made cocktails on the spot according to your tastes at this too-small-to-sit-inside bar. *instagram.com/a_tabacaria; 6pm-2am Sun-Thu, to 3am Fri & Sat*

Pensão Amor
 E7

Popular bar at an old brothel in Cais do Sodré. Come for the signature cocktails and stay to explore the different rooms. *pensaoamor.com; noon-3am*

Live Music

Menina e Moça
52 D7

This laid-back bar and bookshop with jazz jam sessions every Sunday is a happy contrast to Cais do Sodré's noisy bar environment. *instagram.com/meninaemocalivrariabar; 3pm-2am*

Boavista Social Club
 C6

Relaxed bar with frequent jazz and soul sets away from the rowdier central part of Cais do Sodré. *instagram.com/boavista.socialclub; 7pm-2am Tue-Sat*

Beer

Delirium Cafe
 F5

Pub with a good selection of draught beers and friendly service. Arrive early to grab a table on the balcony. *instagram.com/deliriumcafelisboa; 1pm-1am*

Trobadores
55 F6

This medieval-style tavern has wooden tables and beer served in rustic mugs. *facebook.com/TrobadoresBar, noon-12.30am Tue & Wed, to 2am Thu & Fri, 2pm-2am Sat*

Musa da Bica
56 C6

Save the trip to Musa's brewery in Marvila and head to the spin-off bar in Bica to try the latest brews. *cervejamusa.com; 5pm-1am Mon-Thu, 1pm-2am Fri & Sat, to 11pm Sun*

Duque Brewpub
57 E3

Tucked away in the heart of Chiado, Lisbon's first brewpub remains highly recommended for craft beer connoisseurs. *duquebrewpub.com; 4pm-midnight*

Dancing

Incógnito
58 A5

Drink beer and simple cocktails while dancing the night away to '80s and '90s alt rock in The Triangle. Ring the bell to enter. *facebook.com/incognitobar; 11pm-4am Thu-Sat*

Trumps
59 A1

With two dance floors playing house and pop music, this LGBTIQ+ club appeals to a younger crowd. Drag shows on Friday. *trumps.pt; midnight-6am Thu-Sun*

Finalmente
60 B2

Lisbon's first gay nightclub still fills up quickly with customers squeezing in to watch the famous drag shows every night at 3am before dancing the night away. *finalmenteclub.com; midnight-6am*

Capela

 61 D4

The heart of Bairro Alto isn't great for clubbing, unless you're heading here. DJs rarely disappoint, but it gets very crowded on weekends. *facebook.com/acapelabar; 7.30pm-2am Sun-Thu, to 3am Fri & Sat*

Shopping

Fashion
Luvaria Ulisses

 62 F4

This historic shop sells custom-made gloves. Its tiny space welcomes one client at a time. *luvariaulisses.com; 10am-7pm Mon-Sat*

+351

 63 E5

Lisbon-based brand known for its gender-neutral organic cotton clothes. Born in 'The Triangle', it has expanded to more locations, including this shop near Teatro São Carlos. *plus351.pt; 10am-8pm*

Ementa

 64 F5

Streetwear designed by skaters for skaters, this Amadora-born brand started with a group of friends designing custom t-shirts. *ementasb.com; 10am-9pm*

Traces of Me

 65 E4

Committed to slow fashion and sustainability, this female-founded Portuguese ethical designer brand sells colourful garments. *tracesofmetm.com; 10.30am-2pm & 3-7.30pm*

Music & Books
Palavra de Viajante

 66 A5

Nothing but travel and travel-related books in different languages line the shelves of this independent bookstore, organised by geographical areas. *palavra-de-viajante.pt; 10am-2pm & 3-7pm Tue-Sat*

Clube 33

 67 A5

This indie record shop is also a community hub for vinyl collectors and music lovers in The Triangle. *clube33.pt; 11am-7pm Mon-Sat*

Ler Devagar

 68 C2

Comfortable armchairs, antique furniture and a cosy reading nook for kids give a homey vibe to Casa do Comum's bookstore, dedicated to small and independent publishers. *lerdevagar.com; 10am-9pm*

Gourmet Food & Art
Mercearia Poço dos Negros

 69 A5

The whole country seems to fit inside this tiny family-owned grocery store selling artisanal Portuguese products. *instagram.com/merceariapocodosnegros; 10am-8pm Mon-Fri, to 5pm Sat*

Companhia Portugueza do Chá

 70 A5

This tea shop produces its own blends, including the city-inspired Lisbon Breakfast, and is a staple for fans of the brew. *companhiaportuguezadocha.com; 10am-7pm Mon-Sat*

Apaixonarte

 71 A5

This shop sells and showcases art produced by Portugal-based artists. *apaixonarte.com; 11am-7pm Mon-Fri, to 6pm Sat*

Fábrica Sant'Anna

72 E5

In business since 1741, this *azulejo* store and workshop produces artisanal glazed tiles using 300-year-old techniques. *santanna.com.pt; 9.30am-7pm Mon-Fri, from 10am Sat*

See p64
for eating,
drinking and
shopping
listings

VIRTVTIBVS
MAIORVM
VT SIT OMNIBVS DOCVMENTO. P. P. D.

Explore
Baixa & Rossio

When arriving in Lisbon, travellers often head to Baixa first for its spacious squares with black-and-white patterns of *calçada portuguesa* (Portuguese cobblestone pavement) and the golden light bouncing off the Rio Tejo at sunset. Tragedy and renovation mark Lisbon's downtown. After the earthquake of 1755, riverside Baixa followed Marquês de Pombal's rebuilding plan of perfectly laid-out streets – it's an old place that feels new. North of downtown's main street, Rossio still bears the mark of old posh socialite soirées, nights at the theatre and day trips to the countryside of Sintra, despite the high concentration of tourist-centred businesses.

Getting Around

Walking
These mostly flat neighbourhoods are easy to explore on foot. Top attractions are within walking distance from one another.

Metro
The Blue Line covers the area from Terreiro do Paço to Marquês de Pombal. Hop on the metro if you're in a hurry, but avoid rush hour.

Bus
Traffic jams are frequent, and bus travel tends to be slow, even with dedicated lanes. Use it if no other alternatives are available. Bus 711 connects Terreiro do Paço to Marquês de Pombal.

★ THE BEST

VIEWPOINT Arco da Rua Augusta (p61)

ARCHAELOGICAL SITE Núcleo Arqueológico da Rua dos Correeiros (p55)

HISTORIC CAFE Martinho da Arcada (p62)

BAKERY Confeitaria Nacional (p60)

MUSEUM Museu do Design (p59)

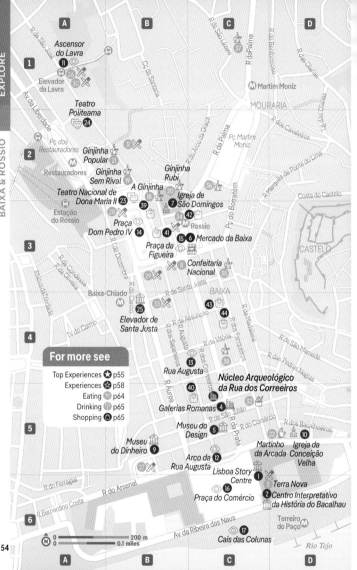

Ascensor do Lavra

Elevador da Lavra

Teatro Politeama

Pç dos Restauradores

Ginjinha Popular

Restauradores

Ginjinha Sem Rival

Ginjinha Rubi

A Ginjinha

Teatro Nacional de Dona Maria II

Igreja de São Domingos

Estação do Rossio

Praça Dom Pedro IV

Rossio

Mercado da Baixa

Praça da Figueira

Confeitaria Nacional

Baixa-Chiado

BAIXA

Elevador de Santa Justa

MOURARIA

Martim Moniz

Costa do Castelo

CASTELO

Rua Augusta

Núcleo Arqueológico da Rua dos Correeiros

Galerias Romanas

Museu do Design

Museu do Dinheiro

Arco da Rua Augusta

Martinho da Arcada

Igreja da Conceição Velha

Lisboa Story Centre

Terra Nova

Praça do Comércio

Centro Interpretativo da História do Bacalhau

Terreiro do Paço

Cais das Colunas

Rio Tejo

For more see

Top Experiences ⭐ p55
Experiences 🟊 p58
Eating 🟉 p64
Drinking 🟢 p65
Shopping 🛍 p65

0 — 200 m
0 — 0.1 miles

54

⭐ TOP EXPERIENCE

Núcleo Arqueológico da Rua dos Correeiros

Halting construction work in Lisbon because of archaeological finds is common. Unveiling 2500 years of history in one go is less frequent, but it happened in the 1990s. Since then, visitors have been guided through the guts of Núcleo Arqueológico da Rua dos Correeiros, discovering secrets of past civilisations.

The Finds

MAP P56, **C5**

The guided tour of the **site** (*fundacaomillennium bcp.pt; free*) starts in a room with interactive maps and blueprints (and praise for the bank-founded foundation that supports the museum). A window shows the building's foundations from three different periods, and the artefacts provide clues as to why Lisbon attracted so many settlers: the fertile river-bed and the abundance of fish. Sardines were the essential raw material for the high-priced *garum* (a fish-based sauce) that Romans exported.

Historical Relics

A narrow staircase takes visitors further into the bowels of the building, where overlapping sub-structures trace Lisbon's past lives as a Phoenician settlement, an Islamic community and part of the Roman Empire, as well as after the 1755 earthquake. Traces of Iron Age hearths, large *garum*-producing tanks, part of an 18th-century sewage system and even a medieval skeleton share the same labyrinthine space.

Ancient Urban Dwellings

The last stop is the remains of a large Roman house built by the side of a former road. From the mezzanine, visitors can see the deep stone vats for warm and cold baths and part of an intact mosaic floor.

PLANNING TIP
Reservations are required by phone or email. Try to book at least a week in advance. Time slots are fixed, with five minutes' tolerance for late arrivals.

Scan this QR code to schedule a free guided tour.

EXPLORE

BAIXA & ROSSIO

Walk Baixa

Perfectly planned streets lead to grand squares of *calçada portuguesa* (Portuguese cobblestone pavement). Stroll through Lisbon's downtown neighbourhood to admire centuries-old shops coexisting with large retail chains. Detour into side streets to find sunset-watching spots and lesser-known historic sites.

START	END	LENGTH
Praça da Figueira	Cais das Colunas	1.75km; 1 hour

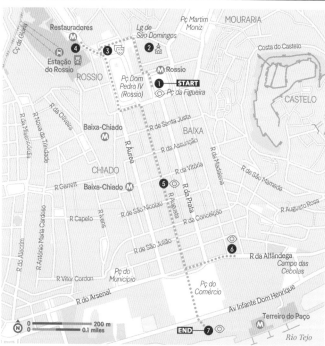

1 Old Hospital

After the 1755 earthquake that wiped out the Baixa and Rossio neighbourhoods, statesman Marquês de Pombal envisioned an organised city. **Praça da Figueira**, downtown's produce market, was built atop the ruins of Hospital de Todos-os-Santos, which the earthquake destroyed. Same-height buildings and cafes line the square.

2 Gruesome Past

A short walk north, the plain facade of **Igreja de São Domingos** hides a dark episode of Portuguese history. It was the starting point of the brutal 1506 Lisbon Massacre, during which thousands of Jewish people were murdered. A memorial honouring the victims rests on the small square outside the church.

3 Portuguese Pavement

Head west to the front terrace at Teatro Nacional de Dona Maria II for a better view of Praça Dom Pedro IV's wavy pavement. Everyone knows the square as just **Rossio**, though. Notice how the pattern of *calçada portuguesa* resembles a sea of black and white cobbles, a tribute to the country's oceanic explorations.

4 Manueline Obsession

See it from afar and then cross the street for a closer look. The facade of **Estação do Rossio** instantly stands out, with decorative elements reminiscent of 15th-century Manueline monuments. But the station was built in the late 1800s, during the Romantic art period when Renaissance and Gothic revival were the trend. In Portugal, the style was called neo-Manueline.

5 Shopping Street

Baixa's main shopping street, pedestrianised **Rua Augusta**, stretches for half a kilometre between Rossio and the mighty Arco da Rua Augusta. Prepare to be engulfed in a sea of enchanted tourists, street performers, loud waiters and annoying scammers trying to pass for 'drug' dealers. It's Lisbon's best and worst side all at once.

6 Old Market

Take a left at the end of Rua Augusta and walk until Rua da Alfândega meets Rua dos Fanqueiros. On the pavement, an almost imperceptible marble slab marks the location of **Largo do Pelourinho Velho**, the 16th-century market where enslaved people were sold. Portugal has yet to acknowledge its active role in the Atlantic slave trade, and Lisbon must work harder to shed light on these places.

7 Sunset Spot

Head back the way you came and cross Praça do Comércio toward **Cais das Colunas**, a place to take a breather and watch the sunset. Resist the appeal of the soft sand and cool Rio Tejo: it's not a beach.

EXPERIENCES

Learn Local History at Lisboa Story Centre · MUSEUM

MAP: **1** P54 **C5**

Before ticking art museums and iconic sights off your list, start at **Lisboa Story Centre** (*lisboastory centre.pt; adult/child €7.50/3.50*). With the audio guide pressed against your ear, move slowly through the rooms, which show videos imagining what life was like during the Phoenician, Roman, Moorish, and pre- and post-earthquake eras. The historical timeline seems to fast forward after that, with quick mentions of the dictatorship years and the democratic revolution that followed, but those topics are better covered elsewhere.

The experience is immersive without being an overwhelming info dump. Even in the room replicating the sensations of the 1755 earthquake and tsunami, the special effects are just a light vibration under your seat and a swinging (well-secured) chandelier above your head.

Find Out All About Salted Cod at História do Bacalhau · MUSEUM

Portugal's obsession with *bacalhau* (salted cod) isn't a mystery, but it's odd that a fish caught in Norway and Iceland became the main ingredient of some of the country's staple dishes. **Centro Interpretativo da História do Bacalhau** (MAP: **2** P54 **D6**; *historiabacalhau.pt; adult/child €4/2*) exists to answer all the questions.

The interactive experience establishes the economic roots of cod fishing, focuses on testimonials of former fishers and even addresses the role of this dish in the dictatorship's propaganda. You can also safely experience the loneliness of being in a tiny boat in the middle of the vast ocean. The visit ends around a virtual table, and the culinary experience can go on next door at **Terra Nova** (MAP: **3** P54 **D6**), the centre's restaurant.

 GALERIAS ROMANAS

Opening only once a year (around 18 April, International Museum Day), **Galerias Romanas** (MAP: **4** P54 **C5**; *museudelisboa.pt; adult/child €3/free*) is a 1st-century CE Roman *crypto portico* (structures built to support large buildings) under Rua da Conceição – and it's Lisbon's most coveted and fleeting attraction. Tickets sell out in the blink of an eye, just minutes after the dates are posted on social media.

Lucky ticket holders descend through a maintenance hole (there are plans to improve access), walk (sometimes slightly hunched) through some of the vaulted galleries supporting Lisbon's downtown and even see one of the fissures caused by the 1755 earthquake.

Explore the Refurbished Museu do Design

MUSEUM

MAP: **5** P54 **C5**

The eight-year wait for Lisbon's **Museu do Design** (*mude.pt; adult/child €11/5.50*) to reopen finally ended in 2024. The guts of the eight-floor former bank are now exposed, making the architecture of this design museum a worthy piece in itself. Floors 3 and 4 are dedicated to the history of Portuguese design with a curated exhibition from MUDE's permanent collections, while floor 5 (Design Labs) is reserved for industry professionals.

Every piece of furniture at MUDE was carefully designed, from the Portuguese-inspired tables and chairs in the 2nd-floor cafe to the restored tile panel in the top-floor restaurant. But the cherry on top is the terrace. The view might not be the best in the city, but the potted sustainable and local plants add a special touch.

Shop at Mercado da Baixa

MARKET

MAP: **6** P54 **C3**

Downtown shop and restaurant owners struggled when shoppers switched from old department stores to more convenient shopping centres. Banding together to improve commerce in the area, they created a business owners' association, which organises

Mercado da Baixa (*adbaixapombalina.pt*) daily in Praça da Figueira (daily) and seasonally in Praça Dom Pedro IV (known as Rossio).

At both locations, small producers have stalls of charcuterie, cheeses, traditional sweets, baked goods, crafts, drinks and *petiscos* (food to share). The **Rossio Christmas Market** is a must-visit event in winter.

Sit Inside Igreja de São Domingos

CHURCH

MAP: **7** P54 **B3**

After walking inside **Igreja de São Domingos** (*free*), it doesn't take long to see the signs of the 1959 fire-blackened walls, broken marble columns, and an absence of the embellishments – apart from the gilded wood carvings decorating the main altar – found in other baroque churches.

But the church has a much darker past – it's where the 1506 Lisbon Massacre started. During Easter, Catholics brutally murdered thousands of New Christians (Jewish people forced to convert to survive) for supposedly causing drought, famine and the Black Plague. A memorial outside the church honours the victims.

Be respectful of the church services, which take place from 8am to noon.

Pause for Coffee & Pastries at Confeitaria Nacional

CAFE

MAP: **8** P54 **B3**

Confeitaria Nacional (*confeitaria nacional.com*) has been at the same address in Praça da Figueira and owned by the same family since it opened in 1829. Today, it's more a whirlwind of tourists than locals, but early mornings are relatively quiet. The staff wear classic black ties and white shirts, taking orders and moving swiftly between tables.

The pace – and the racket – increases throughout the day, and the experience becomes less pleasant during the guided tours' peak hours of 11am to 5pm. If you can't make it outside this time frame, don't let the loud guides talking over one another distract you from admiring the mirrored coffered ceilings and the white wooden cupboards nor from experiencing one of Confeitaria's eclairs (chocolate, caramel or lemon) or the signature *bolo de arroz* (rice muffin).

Discover the Three Reasons to Visit Museu do Dinheiro

MUSEUM

MAP: **9** P54 **B5**

The first reason to head to **Museu do Dinheiro** (*pictured p63; museudodinheiro.pt; free*) is the building: a deconsecrated church bought to expand the Bank of Portugal that's been restored to its original form. Then there's the money and the interactive exhibitions in Portuguese and English about commercial trade and currency. They are cooler for the kids than the grownups, especially touching a gold bar, unless you have a deep interest in the history of cash and banking.

The final reason to visit is the uncovered portion of Lisbon's 13th-century wall. If you're skipping the other two reasons, head down to the lower floor right after the security check. Seeing the wall and the archaeological finds takes less than 20 minutes.

((•)) COMMON SCAMS

Baixa is one of Lisbon's most tourist-heavy areas, which means it attracts plenty of scammers. Selling 'drugs' out in the open – and often under the nose of police officers – is the oldest scam. Portugal decriminalised the use of all illicit drugs in 2001, but decriminalised doesn't mean legal. Scammers take advantage of that misunderstanding, hoping to make quick cash selling fake drugs. Another common scam in this area is 'charities' asking for donations. These volunteers look legit, often wearing lanyards and holding clipboards, but unfortunately, none of the charities exist.

Enter the Surprising Igreja da Conceição Velha
CHURCH

MAP: **⑩** P54 **D5**

In a neighbourhood known for its straight lines and regulated facades, the intricately decorated Manueline-style door of **Igreja da Conceição Velha** *(paroquiasao nicolau.pt; free)* makes those not looking for it stop in their tracks. Some attempt to get the whole church in frame from across the street, practically fusing themselves with the wall while snapping the picture. Eventually, it's best to cross the road to examine all the details up close.

The interior – despite the pink marble walls, baroque paintings and painted stucco ceiling – contrasts with the elaborate entryway. Like other churches that partially survived the 1755 earthquake, this one was rebuilt over centuries, inevitably crossing multiple design styles. One of the few known female artists in 18th-century Portugal, Joana Inácia Rebelo, painted the altarpiece *Nossa Senhora da Pureza* (the middle painting on the right).

View Lisbon from Arco da Rua Augusta
LANDMARK

From the top of **Arco da Rua Augusta** (MAP: **⑫** P54 **C5**; *adult/child €4.50/free*) with your back turned to Rio Tejo, you can see three faces of Lisbon: chaotic but charming Chiado on your left, the tightly knit buildings of Alfama and Castelo de São Jorge on your right, and straight ahead, the carefully planned puzzle piece that is Baixa. Surprisingly, it fits neatly between the other two neighbourhoods. Stores, restaurants and cafes line crowded **Rua Augusta** (MAP: **⑬** P54 **C4**), the main street that connects Baixa to the squares of **Praça Dom Pedro IV** (MAP: **⑭** P54 **B3**) in Rossio and **Praça da Figueira** (MAP: **⑮** P54 **B3**).

On the other side of the *miradouro*, facing the river, see Lisbon's old gateway, the sprawling and bright **Praça do Comércio** (MAP: **⑯** P54 **C6**) and the marble steps and columns of **Cais das Colunas** (MAP: **⑰** P54 **C6**) rising from the water.

 ASCENSOR DO LAVRA

Ascensor do Lavra (MAP: **⑪** P54 **A1**; 1884) is the oldest in Lisbon and was the first street funicular in the world, but it gets a fraction of travellers' attention compared to Bica and Glória, perhaps because the view going up Calçada do Lavra is not the most photo-worthy. If you have spare time, hop on to visit Jardim do Torel and skip the 188m steep walk uphill or just enjoy the historic ride, which takes less than two minutes each way.

Drink Ginjinha, Lisbon's Local Liqueur

BAR

Any time – and any excuse – is suitable for drinking *ginjinha* (sour cherry liqueur). The real deal is served at bar counters in a shot glass, while some bars closer to more touristy areas serve it in an edible chocolate cup.

Established in 1840, **A Ginjinha** (MAP: ⑩ P54 **B2**) claims the habit of drinking sour cherry liqueur started here. Nearby, **Ginjinha Sem Rival** (MAP: ⑰ P54 **B2**) is a popular stop for *ginjinha* or an Eduardino, a fruity drink named after its creator, a regular customer who mixed sour cherry liqueur with anise. Away from Rossio crowds, **Ginjinha Rubi** (MAP: ⑳ P54 **B2**) is a quieter place for *ginjinha*, but space is tight. Admire the *azulejo* (painted glazed tile) panel behind the counter. On a busier Baixa street, **Ginjinha Popular** (MAP: ㉑ P54 **B2**) has higher prices, but drinking a *ginjinha* at the *esplanada* (open-air terrace) is a lifesaver after long hours of sightseeing.

See One of Pessoa's Writing Spots at Martinho da Arcada

CAFÉ

MAP: ㉒ P54 **D5**

Lisbon-born writer Fernando Pessoa (1888–1935), a modernist precursor, lived and worked in Baixa for most of his adult life. He frequently used the city and Rio Tejo as the backdrop of his many alter egos' texts. In *The Book of Disquiet*, his alias Bernardo Soares wrote, 'When one feels too intensely, the Tagus is an endless Atlantic'. Parts of that book and most of the poems included in *Mensagem* (the only of Pessoa's Portuguese poetry books published while he was alive) were written at **Martinho da Arcada**, and his favourite table is forever reserved for him.

The cafe is a tourist attraction, and most visitors stick to quick meals or coffee on the terrace

 THE 1755 LISBON EARTHQUAKE

Almost 300 years later, the Great Lisbon Earthquake is still the city's most talked about event and the one with the most devastating consequences. On the morning of 1 November 1755, Lisbon was devastated by a 7.7 magnitude earthquake followed by a tsunami. A firestorm, caused by the hundreds of candles lit in honour of All Saints' Day, ravaged the city for hours. Lisbon lost an estimated 40,000 people, notable buildings and irreplaceable historical documents. The tragedy influenced 18th-century philosophers, such as Voltaire, and Catholic priests interpreted the event happening on a religious holiday and destroying the city's churches as divine punishment.

despite the inflated prices – no hard feelings if you choose to eat elsewhere and just snap a shot of the cafe's facade.

Go to the Theatre in Rossio
THEATRE

Lisbon hasn't had a bona fide theatre district since Parque Mayer's golden age in the mid-1900s (a cluster of venues off Avenida da Liberdade), but today, the major playhouses concentrate in Rossio.

At 19th-century **Teatro Nacional de Dona Maria II** (MAP: ㉓ P54 **B3**; *tndm.pt*), plays range from reinvented classics to contemporary creations, both national and international. A short walk away, west of Praça Dom Pedro IV, **Teatro Politeama** (MAP: ㉔ P54 **A2**; *filipelaferia.pt*) is the place to go for Portuguese musicals and revue theatre.

Travel in Elevador de Santa Justa
HISTORIC BUILDING

MAP: ㉕ P54 **B4**

The cast-iron structure **Elevador de Santa Justa** *(€6)* opened in 1902 and has been famous ever since. These days, the growing crowds and long queues make it impossible to use as public transportation (its original function), but fortunately, other options bypass the steep uphill walk.

Riding in a unique piece of Lisbon's history compensates for waiting in line. The number of passengers is limited to 20 going up and 15 going down. For fewer crowds, walk up to Carmo (or use the free Carmo Rooftop elevator behind Elevador de Santa Justa) and ride the lift from top to bottom. Although the ticket includes access to the lookout, the top of the lift, from where the views were better, has been closed since 2022.

BREIZHATAO/SHUTTERSTOCK ©

Best Places for...

See p54 for map of locations

Ⓔ Budget ⒺⒺ Midrange ⒺⒺⒺ Top End

Eating

Fine Dining

Solar dos Presuntos
ⒺⒺⒺ

 A1

One of Lisbon's most famous reservations-only, high-end Portuguese cuisine restaurants, with friendly and impeccable service. *solardospresuntos.com; noon-3.30pm & 6.30-11pm Mon-Sat*

Delfina – Cantina Portuguesa ⒺⒺ

27 B5

The restaurant at boutique hotel Alma Lusa embodies the spirit of a typical Portuguese grandma's cuisine, mixing staple dishes with reinventions of traditional recipes. *almalusahotels.com/delfina; noon-4pm & 7-11pm*

Cheap Eats

Beira Gare Ⓔ

28 B3

Popular for cheap sandwiches served at the counter, this is an affordable option for late-night quick meals and a pint. Cash only. *11.30am-10pm Mon-Sat*

Merendinha do Arco Ⓔ

29 B3

Portions are generous at this popular Portuguese food restaurant. Try the speciality *bacalhau à Minhota* (fried cod). *merendinhadoarco.pt; noon-8pm Mon-Fri*

Petiscos

Gracinha ⒺⒺ

30 A1

In Solar dos Presuntos' interior courtyard, a Vhils mural pays tribute to founders Graça and Evaristo. This laid-back restaurant pairs *petiscos* (tapas) and wine with daily cultural events. *gracinha.pt; 6.30pm-12.30am Mon-Sat*

Taberna da Casa do Alentejo Ⓔ

31 B2

This tavern-style casual eatery inside Casa do Alentejo serves food to share from its namesake region in southern Portugal. Save room for traditional desserts. *casadoalentejo.pt/taberna; noon-10.30pm*

Pastries & Ice Cream

Bizarro Gelato Ⓔ

32 C5

Strawberry and olives, peas and basil, and onion and mango are some of the unusual ice-cream flavours you can try here. This place is not afraid to experiment. *instagram.com/bizzarrogelato; noon-7.30pm Tue & Wed, to 11pm Thu-Sun*

Nat'elier Ⓔ

33 B4

This pastry shop in Baixa serves different versions of *pastel de nata,* including traditional or vegan, tiramisu or white chocolate and macadamia nuts, and cookie cheesecake or apple and cinnamon. *natelier.pt; 9am-10pm*

Cafes

Pastelaria Suíça Ⓔ

34 B3

The closure of the original branch of this cafe saddened *lisboetas,* but a couple of years later, a new version opened nearby. The *esquimó* (chocolate-covered cream-filled sponge cake), *duchesse* and *babá* (muffins soaked in rum syrup, with whipped cream filling) pastries remain classics. *paste lariasuica.pt; 8am-11pm*

Drinking

Rooftop Bars

Terraço Editorial

35 C3

On the top floor of the homewares store Pollux, this laid-back bistro serves a selection of Portuguese wines from small producers with views over Baixa. *terracoeditorial.pt; noon-midnight*

Rooftop Bar & Lounge

36 C2

Hotel Mundial's terrace bar is all about the casual atmosphere and the view of Castelo de São Jorge. Toast with the signature Night in Lisbon cocktail. *hotel-mundial. pt; 10.30am-11pm*

Miradouro de Baixo

37 C1

The rooftop bar of cultural centre Carpintarias de São Lázaro puts on frequent live-music con-

certs, DJ sets and other paid events. *instagram .com/miradourodebaixo; 6pm-midnight Fri-Sun*

Cocktails

Imprensa Cocktail & Oyster Bar

38 C4

This tiny bar has named its signature cocktails after fonts, and they pair well with Portuguese oysters. *instagram.com/ imprensa_; 4pm-midnight*

Shopping

Historic Shops

Chapelaria Azevedo Rua

39 B3

The oldest hatmaker in Portugal has been in business since 1886 at the same address in Rossio. *azevedorua.pt; 10am-7pm Mon-Sat*

Casa Pereira da Conceição

40 C5

Go for the decor and architecture and stay for the scent of freshly ground coffee. *10am-10pm*

Manteigaria Silva

41 B3

A family-owned grocery store and one of the top places to buy *bacalhau* and other local delicacies. *manteigariasilva.pt; 9am-7.30pm Mon-Sat*

Hospital de Bonecas

42 C3

Established in 1830, this family-owned doll 'hospital' is also a toy store with a museum upstairs stuffed with vintage dolls and spare parts. *hospitaldebonecas.com; 10am-6pm Mon-Sat*

Vintage

Outra Face da Lua

43 C4

Shop for colourful garments and accessories from the 1960s to the 1990s at one of Lisbon's oldest vintage clothes shops. Sells mostly women's clothes. *aoutrafacedalua.com; 10am-7pm Mon-Fri, from 11am Sat & Sun*

Humana Vintage Secondhand

44 C4

This volunteer and social-work NGO has several shops, and this one in Baixa has a broader selection of vintage clothes. *humana-portu gal.org; 10am-8pm Mon-Sat, from 11am Sun*

See p79
for eating,
drinking and
shopping
listings

Explore
Alfama, Castelo
& Graça

Alfama, Castelo and Graça are known for their sweeping views of the city, clusters of narrow streets and colourful houses cascading downhill towards the Rio Tejo. Alfama and Castelo, the oldest, have seen many versions of Lisbon over the centuries. Parts of these neighbourhoods survived the devastating earthquake, so they are some of the few places with traces of medieval Lisbon. In Graça, a newer neighbourhood that's no less charming, most of the buildings were constructed in the 19th century to accommodate the growing population of factory workers who moved here from other parts of Portugal.

Getting Around

🏃 Walking
Walking is the best way to get around the historic centre, but mind the uneven pavements and slippery cobblestones. Cut distances short using the public free lifts (Elevador do Castelo, Elevador de Santa Luzia) and the Graça funicular.

🚌 Bus
Catch bus 737 from Praça da Figueira to Castelo. Buses 10B (Campo das Cebolas) and 13B (Santa Apolónia) stop near major sights in Alfama and Graça.

Ⓜ Metro
Metro serves Mouraria (Green Line, Martim Moniz exit) and Alfama (Blue Line, Santa Apolónia exit).

★
THE BEST

LIVE MUSIC BAR Damas
(p81)

MUSEUM Museu do Aljube
(p74)

MARKET Feira da Ladra
(p76)

ARCHAEOLOGICAL SITE
Museu do Teatro Romano
(p74)

HISTORIC SITE Igreja da
Graça (p76)

Alfama
KERRY MURRAY/LONELY PLANET ©

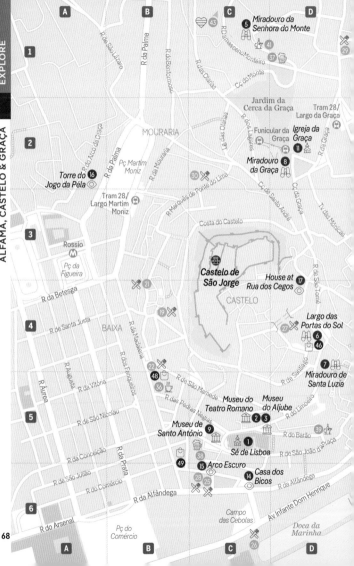

C 43

5 Miradouro da
Senhora do Monte

41

37

D 29

Jardim da
Cerca da Graça

Tram 28/
Largo da Graça

R de São Lázaro

R da Palma

R do Benformoso

MOURARIA

Pç Martim
Moniz

Funicular da
Graça

Igreja da
Graça **11**

Miradouro **8**
da Graça

Torre do **16**
Jogo da Péla

Tram 28/
Largo Martim
Moniz

30

R Marquês de Ponte do Lima

Costa do Castelo

Rossio Ⓜ

Pç da
Figueira

Castelo de
São Jorge

House at **17**
Rua dos Cegos

21

CASTELO

R da Betesga

19

R de Santa Justa

BAIXA

27

Largo das **6**
Portas do Sol **46**

7
Miradouro de
Santa Luzia

22

48

36

R de São Mamede

Museu do
Teatro Romano

Museu
do Aljube

2 **3**

R Áurea

R da Vitória

Museu de
Santo António

9

58

Sé de Lisboa **1**

49

15 Arco Escuro

R de São Nicolau

28 25

14
Casa dos
Bicos

39

R do Barão

R de São João da Praça

R da Alfândega

R da Conceição

R de São Julião

R do Comércio

6

R do Arsenal

Pç do
Comércio

Campo
das Cebolas

26

Av Infante Dom Henrique

Doca da
Marinha

For more see

Top Experiences ⭐ p70
Experiences ✷ p74
Eating ✕ p79
Drinking 🍷 p80
Shopping 🛍 p81

Vila Berta
⑫ ◉

Tv da Pereira

R da Verónica

㊹ ♨

GRAÇA

R da Voz do Operário

Campo de Santa Clara

Campo de
Santa Clara

Feira da
Ladra ⑩ ㊲ ⑱ Panteão
Nacional

Arco Grande de Cima

㊺ ♨

㊳ ♫ ㉞ ♫

R do Paraíso

⑳

R do Museu de Artilharia

Santa Apolónia
Train Station

Santa
Apolónia Ⓜ

Escolas Gerais

♫ ㉝ ㉜ ♫

㊺ ♨

R do Vigário

ALFAMA

R dos Remédios

R do Jardim do Tabaco

R de São Miguel

㊵

⑬ Museu
do Fado

R Terreiro do Trigo

④ ✷
Jewish Lisbon Walking
Tour

Rio Tejo

Ⓝ 0 ———————— 500 m
0 ———————— 0.25 miles

E F G H

★ TOP EXPERIENCE

Castelo de São Jorge

Cosmetic repairs aside, Castelo de São Jorge precedes Portugal as a country. The castle is more than a medieval defence fort. Within its walls lived Lisbon's first civilisations and royal families. Roam the snaking ramparts and shaded courtyards for views over the city's red rooftops.

MAP P68, **C3**

PLANNING TIP
Visit in the morning to avoid crowds and buy your tickets online in advance. Ticket holders have a dedicated line, so you'll spend less time waiting to go inside.

Scan this QR code for opening hours and to buy tickets.

Views of the City

Many visitors come to the **castle** (castelodesao jorge.pt; adult/child €15/free) for its views over Lisbon. It's undoubtedly one of the best lookouts, and it's rarely crowded (what a gift!). Reactions to the view vary from a loud yelp to a quiet jaw drop – it never disappoints.

Towers & Interior

After admiring the view, go up to the **Jardim Romântico** and try to figure out which of the stones were part of the now ruined Paço Real (royal palace). Continue to the castle, explore every inch of the walls and the towers, and stop at every opportunity to take another look at Lisbon from above. Mind the irregular pavement. It's a medieval castle, after all, so the stones are uneven and slippery. Some of the stairs are high, and the paths have dents and smooth surfaces from all who have walked here before.

Every part of Castelo de São Jorge is worth exploring, but think twice before climbing down the steep and uneven stairsteps to **Torre de São Lourenço**. It will be a challenging climb up. Take your time if you're uncomfortable with heights.

RTEM/SHUTTERSTOCK ©

Historical Sites

The archaeological site is the last stop before leaving, but it is an important one to fully grasp all of Lisbon's historical layers. Over the years, several excavations revealed remains belonging to three different periods and civilisations: a 7th-century BCE kitchen (Iron Age), traces of an 11th-century CE Islamic quarter and ruins of a 16th-century palace for the bishops. It takes a little imagination to make sense of the ruins, but it helps to visit the permanent exhibition between the romantic garden and the castle before heading to the archaeological site.

QUICK BREAK
Refuel with a snack at **Lovely Castelo** (the red kiosk near the entrance). For a more substantial meal, head to its restaurant with a view.

🚶 WALKING TOUR

Walk Alfama, Castelo & Graça

Wander the historic centre's narrow cobblestone streets and spot yellow trams wobbling up and down the hill, buildings covered in chipped *azulejos* (painted glazed tiles), tuk-tuk drivers advertising 'unmissable' deals, and tourists interrupting old ladies gossiping on doorsteps to buy a shot of *ginjinha* from them.

START	END	LENGTH
Centro Comercial Mouraria	Chafariz d'El Rei	2.25km; 1½ hours

1 Neighbourhood Shopping

Always busy, **Centro Comercial da Mourari**a is the go-to spot for spices in bulk, Asian food staples and bargains. Even if shopping isn't in your plan, browse the five floors of Mouraria's multiethnic commercial heart to see the wide range of stuff for sale.

2 Fado Street

Across the pavement, **Mouraria – Berço do Fado**, a sculpture honouring fado, marks the beginning of Rua do Capelão, where this music genre was supposedly born. Notice the photos of prominent *fadistas* (fado singers) decorating the walls, a work by artist Camilla Watson.

3 Secluded Square

Continue east to **Largo da Severa**, a quiet square off the crowded streets of central Mouraria named after the first *fadista*. The silence is disturbed only by the occasional group of wandering tourists or neighbours catching up.

4 Street Art

Continue up the maze of cobblestoned streets to Rua dos Lagares. Walk up the zigzagging staircases known as Caracol da Graça and admire street art on the way. On hot days, cut the walk short and ride the Graça funicular instead.

5 Break with a View

Take a break at **Miradouro da Graça** and admire Lisbon's colourful buildings stretching towards Rio Tejo under the always-watchful Castelo de São Jorge atop the hill. This excellent view requires a longer stay, so sit with a drink at Esplanada da Graça and relax.

6 Workers' Blocks

Cross Jardim da Graça and notice the blue-green tiled building on the right, with the sign **Villa Sousa**. It's one of the old factory workers' blocks built by industrialists to house migrants from elsewhere in the country to work in Lisbon. Continue on Largo da Graça for the more picturesque village-within-the-city block of **Vila Berta**.

7 Old Jewish Quarter

Walk southeast on Rua da Voz do Operário to Portas do Sol and head downstairs. The winding alleyways and stairs lead to the heart of the old **Jewish Quarter** at Largo de São Miguel. The only signs left of the quarter are the street name (Rua da Judiaria) and the old gate at the medieval wall, Cerca Velha, next to Centro Cultural Judaico.

8 Water Fountain

Next, head to **Chafariz d'El Rei**, one of the most beautiful public water fountains in Alfama and the first in the city (no longer in use). The facade was added to the original 13th-century structure in the late 1800s, with nine spouts – used by different genders and social classes – of which you can see three.

73

EXPERIENCES

Step Inside the Medieval Sé de Lisboa
CHURCH

MAP: **1** P68 **C5**

Sé de Lisboa (*sedelisboa.pt; adult/ child €5/3*) doesn't go unnoticed on the side of the street leading up to Alfama's *miradouros* (viewpoints). Although most admire the medieval church from the outside, behind its austere facade are high vaulted ceilings, stained-glass windows and a small museum of religious art worth visiting.

Archaeological excavations in the cloisters have closed them to sightseers for three decades, but they are expected to reopen in 2025. Those in a rush or on a budget can enter for free, but without paying, you aren't allowed beyond the dozen or so pews in the back of the church. It's not the best experience but not the worst of views either.

Visit Roman Ruins at Museu do Teatro Romano
MUSEUM

MAP: **2** P68 **C5**

In Lisbon, Roman ruins are scarce and scattered, most buried underneath the rubble of the 1755 earthquake and the foundations of the rebuilt city, waiting to be discovered during the construction of a new building or underground car park.

In Alfama, the ruins of a 1st-century CE theatre led to the opening of **Museu do Teatro Romano** (*museudelisboa.pt; adult/child €3/free*). Although the museum's artefact collection is worth the one-hour visit, the old playhouse outdoors draws most of the attention, and it's free admission. An open-air archaeological excavation that began in the late 1960s is one of the country's most important historical finds – in Portugal, only Lisbon and Braga had Roman theatres.

Learn About Portugal's Recent Past at Museu do Aljube
MUSEUM

MAP: **3** P68 **C5**

Museu do Aljube (*museudoaljube. pt; adult/child €3/free*) tells the story of one of the darkest periods of Portugal's recent history: the conservative dictatorship known as the Estado Novo and the fight for democracy that culminated with

 JEWISH LISBON WALKING TOUR

While traces of Roman and Islamic civilisations are well documented and relatively easy to locate, the Jewish presence in Lisbon is often mentioned in connection with tragic events, such as the 1506 massacre. The guided **Jewish Lisbon Walking Tour** (MAP: **4** P68 **E5**; *judiarialisboa.com; €50*), a project by Centro Cultural Judaico, has started to close that gap. The three-hour tour (in English or Hebrew) through the heart of Alfama provides historical, cultural and social context.

the peaceful military coup on 25 April 1974.

Set inside the former political prison where regime opponents were jailed and tortured, the museum gives a punch-in-the-gut account of nearly five decades of totalitarianism and the colonial agenda that supported it. Personal testimonies, documents and photos of those who perished at the hands of the political police trace the timeline of these events that took place not so long ago.

See the View from Popular Lookouts VIEWPOINT

Miradouros in the historic centre are a dime a dozen, but we're just accounting for the four official ones, which are also free to visit. From windy **Miradouro da Senhora do Monte** (MAP: **5** P68 C1) between Graça and Mouraria, you can see Praça Martim Moniz, parts of downtown and the winding street of Calçada do Monte that takes you down to the heart of Mouraria.

Largo das Portas do Sol (MAP: **6** P68 D4) in Alfama is all about drinks in the sun at the outdoor cafe looking over the Rio Tejo. Less than 100m down the street, **Miradouro de Santa Luzia** (MAP: **7** P68 D4) renders the view romantic with its tile panels and pergola. **Miradouro da Graça** (MAP: **8** P68 D2) is the city's timeless terrace where you can watch Lisbon wind down as the sun sets. Expect crowds throughout the day.

Get to Know Lisbon's Patron Saint at Museu de Santo António MUSEUM

MAP: **9** P68 C5

Museu de Santo António (*museu delisboa.pt; adult/child €3/free*) is dedicated to Lisbon's favourite patron saint (though the official saint is São Vicente). This museum shows works with references to the saint in historical documents, literature and pop culture. However, the colourful art installation of flowers and the statue outside seem to appeal more to people than the exhibitions inside.

The museum organises special events around Valentine's Day in honour of St Anthony's alleged talent as *santo casamenteiro* (matchmaker saint). According to local lore, if you throw a coin at the statue and it lands on the open book, it's a sign that true love is in the air.

Celebrate Santos Populares FESTIVAL

Lisbon's most famous street celebrations are the summertime *santos populares*. In honour of St Anthony and St Vincent, Lisbon's historic neighbourhoods fill up with a beer-holding, sardine-eating crowd (plant-based options are not easy to find, but not impossible), usually dancing the night away to a particular Portuguese music genre known as *música pimba* (flashy dancers, high-pitched singers and tunes that mix pop with a folksy beat).

That's the top daily (or rather, nightly) activity in June, peaking on the 12 June, the eve of Lisbon's holiday. The feast spreads across the city, but it's strongest in Alfama, Graça and Mouraria, and these neighbourhoods burst at the seams with merrymakers. Grab a table at one of the *arraiais* (street parties) and join locals for a dinner of grilled sardines, boiled potatoes and roasted peppers.

Over the last decade, most of the *arraiais* have evolved from purely neighbourhood-based celebrations to branded social events that welcome all music genres. Arraial da Mouraria, organised by local NGO **Renovar a Mouraria** (*renovar amouraria.pt*), remains one of the few *arraiais* where socialising and celebrating are still the top priority.

Shop for Bargains at Feira da Ladra

MARKET

MAP: P68 **F3**

Campo de Santa Clara is home to Lisbon's oldest flea market, and it has become the city's most popular when it takes place on Tuesday and Saturday. Feira da Ladra is a mix of professional vendors, with proper stalls displaying vintage merchandise and handcrafts, and occasional sellers with blankets full of scattered objects on the pavement. Finding the treasures among the clutter is an exercise in patience, but shoppers won't leave empty-handed.

Early Saturday mornings are best for browsing. Bring cash and get ready to negotiate.

Discover the Multiple Sides of Igreja da Graça

CONVENT

MAP: ⑪ P68 **D2**

When visitors head to Miradouro da Graça (p75) for that classic view over Lisbon, 13th-century **Igreja da Graça** (*igrejadagraca. pt; adult/child €5/free*) is often an afterthought. But a glance past the doorway is all it takes to wonder if the interior of this baroque convent is as beautiful as those marble floors and walls. You find out that it

⚠ STOLEN AZULEJOS

Selling historic *azulejos* (painted glazed tiles) is a lucrative business. The rarer the piece, the higher the profit, which leads to criminal activity, and the Portuguese police have a division dedicated to investigating tile theft (sosazulejo.com). A lot of Lisbon's old building facades are missing dozens of *azulejos*, most of them carefully removed from the walls. The closer the gaps are to the ground, the more likely it is they were stolen. They are often sold later at Feira da Ladra, street markets or antique stores to unsuspecting tourists. Movement **MAPA** (facebook.com/azulejo. patrimonio.em.risco) does a good job of raising awareness about this issue.

is while roaming through *azulejo*-covered rooms and admiring the church's art and pink marble walls.

Capitalising on the terrace's possibilities and in need of funding, this Catholic convent moved up a notch in the tourist attraction department and opened a rooftop *miradouro* in 2023. More than a convent and piece of local heritage, Igreja da Graça is now a must-visit cultural space. The upper cloister doubles as an art gallery, the noble hall plays host to concerts, and the cloisters become an **outdoor cinema** *(theblackcatcinema.com)* in summer.

Find Traces of Graça's Workers' Quarters
STREET

MAP: **12** P68 **E1**

In the early 20th century at the peak of industrialisation in Lisbon and the consequent population increase, factory workers' neighbourhoods proliferated in the city to accommodate migrants from other parts of the country. These small clusters of houses known as *vilas* (villages) were a quarter within a quarter, sometimes more of a private block of flats with an interior courtyard (Vila Sousa at Largo da Graça is a good example of that).

Vila Berta, a short walk from Largo da Graça, is a picturesque quiet side street with cute, same-style houses with tiles and wrought-iron balconies. This for-mer factory workers' block is also one of Graça's popular places for the annual street celebrations in honour of the city's popular saints (p75).

At Bairro Estrela d'Ouro, another of these industrial blocks in Rua da Graça, the only thing left is the tile panel on the wall.

Learn About Lisbon's Urban Song at Museu do Fado
MUSEUM

MAP: **13** P68 **E5**

The roots of fado run deep in Lisbon's old quarters. Nowadays, this sorrowful music genre is more associated with the Alfama neighbourhood, but it was born in Mouraria's *tascas*. It went from working-class entertainment to a famous world-music genre in what feels like a heartbeat.

Before heading to a *casa de fado* (a traditional restaurant where *fadistas* sing at regular intervals between courses at dinner) or discarding the genre, understand its nuanced history at **Museu do Fado** *(museudofado.pt; adult/child €5/free)*.

Learn about several generations of artists; listen to their songs; admire the different types of *guitarra portuguesa* (Portuguese guitar), a crucial instrument of the genre; and see *O Fado* (1910), Jose Malhoa's portrait of two neighbourhood characters: *fadista* Amâncio and his mistress Adelaide.

See Archaeological Finds & a Nobel Prize at Casa dos Bicos
NOTABLE BUILDING

MAP: **14** P68 **C6**

The 1st floor of the 16th-century Renaissance-style **Casa dos Bicos** houses **Fundação José Saramago** (*josesaramago.org; adult/child €3/ free*), the foundation dedicated to the namesake Portuguese author and winner of the Nobel Prize for Literature in 1998. This building at Campo das Cebolas has a peculiar facade covered in diamond-shaped stones and neo-Moorish window frames. Inside, visitors have access to a diverse repository of the writer's career, including photos, personal calendars and notebooks, annotated manuscripts, books translated into different languages, and, of course, his Nobel medal.

Whether or not you're visiting the small museum upstairs, don't skip seeing the archaeological findings on the ground floor (free): ancient Roman tanks used to process fish, remains of the Moorish city walls and a portion of the 14th-century city walls.

PRE-1755 EARTHQUAKE CONSTRUCTION

Arco Escuro

MAP: **15** P68 **C6**

Now used as a shortcut to reach Sé de Lisboa (p74), the archway leading to the namesake alley is the old gateway Porta do Mar from the first pre-13th century city wall, Cerca Velha.

Torre do Jogo da Péla

MAP: **16** P68 **A2**

West of Praça Martim Moniz, you can see part of the 14th-century city wall, Cerca Fernandina. At first glimpse, it looks like fragile left-overs from a construction site.

House at Rua dos Cegos

MAP: **17** P68 **D4**

Lisbon's oldest house, built in the 1500s, is at the corner of this Alfama street.

Pay Tribute to Portugal's Greatest at Panteão Nacional
MUSEUM

MAP: **18** P68 **G3**

Panteão Nacional (*panteao nacional.gov.pt; adult/child €8/ free*) took 400 years to complete. The church's dome was the last feature added (1966), and it's the first feature that grabs your attention from afar, followed by the wavy facade. Inside, your eyes are drawn to the dome's interior, the main chapel's organ and the pattern of the marble floors (get a better view from the high choir).

It's the final resting place of some of the country's most prominent personalities, and you can visit the tombs of football star Eusébio, fado diva Amália, presidents, politicians and distinguished authors on the ground floor.

Best Places for...

$** Budget **$$** Midrange **$$$ Top End

See p68 for map of locations

EXPLORE

ALFAMA, CASTELO & GRAÇA

Eating

Contemporary Portuguese

O Velho Eurico $$
 B4

Named after the former owner, this *tasca*, run by young chefs since 2018, serves classics like *bacalhau* (salted cod) and octopus. *instagram.com/ovelhoeurico; 12.30-3pm & 8-10.30pm Tue-Sat*

Taberna Albricoque $$
20 G3

This quiet, chef-owned restaurant in Santa Apolónia serves Algarve-inspired seafood dishes and Alentejo-inspired *petiscos* (tapas). *instagram.com/taberna.albricoque; 7-11pm Tue, noon-3pm & 7-11pm Wed-Sat*

Tasca Baldracca $$
21 B4

This small and unassuming restaurant in Mouraria is proof that fusion cuisine with Portuguese inspiration is welcome at a *tasca. instagram.com/tascabaldracca; 12.30-3pm & 8-11pm Tue-Sat*

Cheap & Traditional Portuguese

As Bifanas do Afonso $
22 B4

Locals and travellers queue for the popular *bifana* (pork sandwich), but none of the sandwiches on the menu disappoint. *8am-6.30pm Mon-Fri, 9am-1.30pm Sat*

Sardinha $
23 F4

Owned by a wife-and-husband team, this small restaurant in Alfama offers love in every dish. The owners are the only staff, so disregard the slow service. *9.30am-midnight Mon-Fri, from 7pm Sun*

Maçã Verde $
24 G3

Traditional, no-frills Portuguese restaurant steps away from Santa Apolónia station. Check the handwritten menus for the day's specials. *noon-3pm & 7-11pm Mon-Fri, noon-3pm Sat*

Fine Dining

Sála $$$
25 C6

Chef João Sá's restaurant with one Michelin star and two seafood tasting menus is a culinary oasis among the overpriced tourist-trap restaurants near Campo das Cebolas. *restaurantesala.pt; 6.30-9.30pm Tue-Thu, 12.30-2pm & 6.30-10.30pm Fri & Sat*

ÀCosta by Olivier $$$
26 C6

Classic Portuguese dishes get a contemporary spin at this riverside restaurant. Seafood rules the menu, though other options are available. *acostabyolivier.pt; 12.30-3pm & 7-11pm Sun & Tue-Thu, to 11.30pm Fri & Sat*

Grenache $$$
27 D4

At this Michelin-starred restaurant, chef Philippe Gelfi created two tasting menus where Portuguese dishes meet French cooking techniques. *grenache.pt; 7.30-10.30pm Thu-Mon*

Breakfast & Brunch

Basílio

28 C6

Decorated with bright colours, this cosy all-day breakfast spot is a popular cafe in Alfama. Go for the fixed brunch menu if you can't decide between pancakes or eggs. *ilovenicolau.com; 8am-5pm Mon-Thu, to 7pm Fri-Sun*

Maria Limão

29 D1

Female-founded business that went from a lemonade cart at the Senhora do Monte lookout to a brick-and-mortar brunch restaurant in central Graça. The berry-stuffed pancakes are a must-try. *instagram .com/bebemarialimao; 9am-6pm Mon-Fri, to 7pm Sat & Sun*

Vegan & Vegetarian

Food Temple

30 C2

At this vegan restaurant in Mouraria, the outdoor staircase doubles as seats and tables, but head inside for a more comfortable experience. Order the tasting menu to try all the dishes. *thefoodtemple.com; 6.30-11.30pm Tue-Sun*

Santa Clara dos Cogumelos

31 F2

It's not all about mushrooms despite this vegetarian-friendly restaurant's name, but the fungi are a star ingredient. *santaclaradoscogumelos. com; 7.30-11pm Sun-Fri, 1-3.30pm & 7.30-11pm Sat*

Food & Fado

Tasca da Bela

32 F4

This small and famous fado haunt in Alfama fills up fast. Recommended for late-night *petiscos* if you can grab a table. *facebook.com/ bela.vinhosepetiscos; 8pm-4am Tue-Sun*

Mesa de Frades

33 F4

At this former chapel turned cosy restaurant in Alfama, the roster of *fadistas* includes newcomers and established performers. *instagram .com/mesadefrades; 8.30pm-2am Mon-Sat*

O Corrido

34 F3

This family-owned business away from the *casas de fado* in Alfama offers an authentic and affordable experience. *ocorrido.com; 7.30-11pm Sun & Tue-Thu, to midnight Fri & Sat*

Drinking

Cafes

Hello, Kristof

35 F3

Home of great coffee and independent magazines. This cosy cafe has its second location in Alfama near Panteão Nacional. *hellokristof.com; 9am-4pm*

Paleio Cafe

36 B5

This cute and colourful cafe with friendly staff has a designated area for laptop users in case you want a change of scenery while working. *instagram .com/paleio.cafe; 8am-7pm Tue-Sun*

Craft Beer

8ª Colina

37 D1

At Oitava Colina's taproom in Graça, you can try the Portuguese brand's best-selling artisanal brews, new creations and seasonal limited-production beers. *oitavacolina.pt; 4-11pm Sun-Thu, to 1am Fri & Sat*

Outro Lado

38 C5

Try more than 300 Portuguese and international artisanal beers at this bar tucked away in a quasi-hidden alley in Alfama. *outrolado.beer; 5-11pm Sun, Wed, & Thu, to 2am Fri & Sat*

Cocktails & Wine

The Terrace
 D5

One of the first rooftop bars before the trend hit Lisbon, The Terrace is the perfect spot for casual drinks with views over Alfama. *memmohotels. com; noon-11pm*

Ulysses Speakeasy
 E4

This reservations-only, almost-secret microbar in the heart of Alfama is famous for its customised cocktails. *instagram.com/ UlyssesLisbon; 4pm-midnight Sat-Tue*

L'APE Italian Lounge
 C1

Enjoy the Italian tradition of aperitivo at this casual bar and restaurant near Miradouro Senhora do Monte with Italian appetisers, wines and bottled beers. *instagram .com/lapeitalianlounge; noon-11pm*

Dancing

Lux-Frágil
 H3

Lisbon's hottest nightclub is selective and a favourite for drinks with live music and dancing

until dawn. *luxfragil.com; midnight-6am Thu-Sun*

Live Music & Events

Drama Bar
 C1

LGBTIQ+ bar and cultural venue hosting drag shows, lip-syncing events and extravagant theme parties. *instagram .com/dramabar.lisboa; 7pm-midnight Wed-Sun*

Damas
 E2

Graça's eclectic alternative concert hall in an old bakery. Check the weekly cocktail menu on the tiled walls. *instagram.com/ damas.lisboa; noon-4am Fri & Sat*

Típica de Alfama
 E4

Alfama isn't just about fado – check out this tiny family-owned bar with eclectic live acts. *instagram.com/ tipicadealfama; 7pm-2am Mon-Sat*

Shopping

Ceramics

XVIII Azulejo e Faiança
 D4

Specialises in hand-painted *azulejos* pro-

duced using 18th-century techniques. Watch the artisans at work. *xviii.pt; 10am-7pm Mon-Sat*

Cerâmica São Vicente
 E3

Family-owned ceramics shop selling handmade and hand-painted *azulejos* and other pieces. Book a workshop to take a unique souvenir home. *ceramica-svicentelisboa. com; 11am-4pm Tue-Fri, to 5pm Sat*

Souvenirs

Madalena à Janela
 B4

This shop is a tribute to the owners' love for Portuguese-made arts and crafts. Shop for ethical and local ceramics, tote bags and t-shirts. *madajanela.com; 10.30am-7.30pm Mon-Fri, to 7pm Sat*

Conserveira de Lisboa
 B6

Getting that can of sardines with your birth year from the flashy souvenir shop is cute, but it doesn't beat the family-like customer service at this historic shop. *conserveirade lisboa.pt; 10am-7pm Mon-Sat*

See p94
for eating,
drinking and
shopping
listings

Explore
Belém

As the port from which Portuguese navigators set sail, Belém is forever linked to the age of sea exploration. The prosperous 'finds' of that era made Portugal one of the wealthiest countries in Europe, and profits were used to build grand monuments, such as Mosteiro dos Jerónimos. The palaces and manors of aristocrats and monarchs who spent their summers here in the 18th century are now museums, embassies and public buildings. Belém is busy during the day, but after tourists have returned to the city centre in the evening, the neighbourhood becomes quiet and empty despite being one of Lisbon's busiest cultural centres.

Getting Around

🚶 Walking
Belém is flat, and all major sights are within walking distance of one another, so exploring on foot is the best option.

🚲 Bicycle
The riverside cycling path is one of the best in Lisbon. Find a Gira bike-share station near Torre de Belém and another near MAAT.

🚍 Bus
Riding the bus is not the fastest option, but it could be a good choice. Bus 727 connects Mosteiro dos Jerónimos to MAAT. Bus 728 goes from Jerónimos to Belém's ferry station.

★
THE BEST

GARDEN Jardim Botânico Tropical (p88)

HERITAGE SITE Mosteiro dos Jerónimos (p86)

MUSEUM MAAT Gallery (p93)

PASTRIES Pastéis de Belém (p93)

VIEWPOINT Padrão dos Descobrimentos (p88)

Torre de Belém (p85)
DMITRY RUKHLENKO/SHUTTERSTOCK ©

For more see

Top Experiences ⭐ p85
Experiences 🔲 p88
Eating 🍴 p94
Drinking 🍷 p95
Shopping 🛍 p95

Palácio Nacional da Ajuda 5

Museu do Tesouro Real 7

Jardim Botânico da Ajuda 6

Cc da Tapada

Cc da Ajuda

RESTELO

Av Ilha da Madeira

Av do Restelo

Av Rainha Dona Amélia

R dos Jerónimos

R Dom Francisco de Almeida

R Dom Francisco de Almeida

R Tristão da Cunha

R Dom Cristóvão da Gama

R Pedrouços

Av da Índia

Av do Brasília

Av Dom Vasco da Gama

R do Alto do Duque

Av das Descobertas

Jardim Botânico Tropical 1

Antigo Picadeiro Real

Mosteiro dos Jerónimos ◎

Pastéis de Belém

Pc do Império

Museu de Arte Contemporânea MAC/CCB 8

Centro Cultural de Belém

Museu Nacional dos Coches 🏛

Estação Fluvial de Belém

Quake 🏛 Belém 12

MAAT 16
MAAT 17 Central
MAAT Garden 21 15
MAAT Gallery 🏛

Rio Tejo

Padrão dos Descobrimentos 2

Doca de Belém

Museu de Arte Popular 9

Doca do Bom Sucesso

Torre de Belém 🗼

R da Junqueira

0   500 m
0   0.25 miles

84

 ★ **TOP EXPERIENCE**

Torre de Belém

A UNESCO World Heritage Site since 1983, the Manueline-style Torre de Belém is one of Lisbon's most recognisable symbols. Step inside this city gateway for a closer look at its intricately decorated interior and see Belém from the top of the 16th-century defence tower.

The Terrace

After crossing the wooden bridge from the river-bank to the **tower** *(museusemonumentos.pt; adult/child €8/free)* and getting closer to its distinctive decor, the ground floor probably feels disappointing with its bare stone walls and cannons. But the experience quickly improves when you climb the first set of stairs (be careful on the uneven stones) to the terrace on the 1st floor. This is where visitors spend the most time, noticing the detailed stonework and taking in the views of the city and Rio Tejo.

Inside the Tower

Inside the four-floor structure, the rooms feel bare compared to the tower's exterior, but each has something unique to notice. Admire the marble floors in each room, step onto the balcony in the king's chamber (2nd floor) and look up at the high vaulted ceilings in the chapel (4th floor).

Top of the Tower

As you make your way up, sit by the windows in each room to rest from climbing the 93-step spiral staircase (steep and a little narrow) through the four floors. The end of the journey comes with rewarding views from the top terrace.

MAP P84, **B4**

PLANNING TIP
Visit in the morning after Mosteiro dos Jerónimos. Lines move fast, but plan to wait for at least 30 minutes. If time is short, visit only the rampart's terrace.

Scan this QR code for opening hours.

★ **TOP EXPERIENCE**

Mosteiro dos Jerónimos

The massive Mosteiro dos Jerónimos is one of Lisbon's best-known examples of Manueline architecture, impressive in size and decor. King Manuel I wanted the monastery to represent the success of the Portuguese overseas explorations and the country's foreseeable control of the spice trade sea route.

MAP P84, **C3**

PLANNING TIP
Early mornings are the best time to visit, but expect to queue for at least 30 minutes. Buy tickets from the official website to save a trip to the ticket office.

Scan this QR code for opening hours and to buy tickets.

Cloisters

Everywhere around the two-floor cloisters of this **monastery** (*museusemonumentos.pt; adult/child €12/free*), you notice rope-like elements, maritime creatures (a nod to sea exploration) and the armillary sphere (used by King Manuel I and became the symbol of the Portuguese empire) on the intricately decorated Mudejar-style arches and columns.

On the ground floor, after the 12 confessionals, an elaborate doorway marks the entrance to the **Chapter Room**, where the tomb of historian and Romantic author Alexandre Herculano (1810–77) draws your attention. The interior was decorated only in the late 1800s when the Neo-Manueline Revival style was in fashion. It's curious to see both styles under the same roof, and it's practically impossible to tell the difference.

Portals

It's difficult to properly appreciate the **West Portal**, the church's main entrance, because when you're close enough to see every detail, the line starts moving faster and visitors are ushered inside the monastery. However, on the way out, you can spend a couple of minutes admiring the stonework if it's not crowded and staff aren't trying to move people along. Despite being a side entrance, the **South Portal** is even more impressive. Built by hundreds of

BENNY MARTY/SHUTTERSTOCK ©

stonemasons and artists over two years in the 1500s, it's considered a late Gothic masterpiece.

The Church

With a dedicated queue (opposite the line for ticket holders) for visitors who want to see the church only (free entry), **Igreja de Santa Maria de Belém** is a mashup of several renovations over the centuries on top of the original Manueline structure of rope-like columns decorated with fruit, sea creatures and armillary spheres. The tombs of 16th-century poet Luís de Camões (on the right side of the entrance) and explorer Vasco da Gama (on the left), elaborate frescoes in the main altar, stained-glass windows (a 1940s addition), and rich marble floors contrast with the stark stone walls and high ceilings.

QUICK BREAK
Refuel at **Pastéis de Belém** across the street after your visit with one (or six) freshly baked creamy custard tarts sprinkled with cinnamon and powdered sugar.

EXPERIENCES

Take a Breather at Jardim Botânico Tropical

GARDENS

MAP: ❶ P84 **D3**

Behind Pastéis de Belém (p93) is a not-so-secret 7-hectare tropical garden refuge. At **Jardim Botânico Tropical** (*museus.ulisboa.pt; adult/child €5/free*), the only (often loud) distractions are the resident peacocks roaming among humans.

After the ticket office, visitors can take the first path on the right, lined with palm trees, a lake and perfectly manicured lawns, but those with a more adventurous spirit often take the path on the left, which leads to the Asian garden. It's a haven of tall trees and streams and ponds crossed by red bridges, with a pagoda-style sitting area (admittedly in need of upkeep) near the exit.

The tropical garden has trees and plants from all over the world, plus a handful of busts depicting the indigenous populations of Portugal's African and Asian colonies, built for the 1940 Portuguese World Exhibition, a nationalist event for the dictatorship. However, there is no information or context given on-site about the peculiar choice of 'decor'.

See Belém from the Top of Padrão dos Descobrimentos

MONUMENT

MAP: ❷ P84 **C4**

The massive white stone monument of **Padrão dos Descobrimentos** (*padraodosdescobrimentos.pt; adult/child €10/5*) was commissioned during the Estado Novo dictatorship for the 1940 Portuguese World Exhibition and depicts the bow of a Portuguese caravel, with prominent figures from the 'Age of Discovery' aboard. It's an undeniably beautiful work, but its connection to sea exploration as a feat of greatness (common propaganda during the dictatorship, but one that needs revision today) has made the monument a target of protests and vandalism.

Nevertheless, visitors come for the view, the best in Belém. Don't miss the exhibitions on the lower ground floor; curators are working to shed light on sensitive topics, such as racism, the dictatorship's propaganda and colonialism.

Cross the River to Trafaria

BOAT TRIP

Hop on the ferry from **Estação Fluvial de Belém** (MAP: ❸ P84 **E4**) to **Trafaria** (MAP: ❹ P84 **E4**; *ttsl.pt; €1.45*) to see Belém from Rio Tejo's south bank. Departures are every hour, and the small town is just 20 minutes away.

When you reach the other side, exit the station to the right and go toward the seaside pedestrian-only walking path with colourful houses, restaurants and cafes. A wall separates the path from the small beach below, with fishing boats anchored at the bay between this stretch of sand and the Trafaria harbour. Look across the river (Belém is on the right) and take in the view.

Visit the Last Royal Palace, Palácio Nacional da Ajuda   PALACE

MAP: **5** P84 **E1**

If the proportions of **Palácio Nacional da Ajuda** *(palacioajuda. gov.pt; adult/child €8/4)* seem off when you step inside the interior courtyard, your eyes aren't deceiving you. After the Portuguese royal family was forced to seek exile in Brazil following French invasions in 1807, construction stopped and never resumed.

Inside, the explosion of frescoes, tapestries, heavy velvet drapes and silk-covered walls quickly overrides the thought of being inside a half-finished palace. It's hard to weigh the importance of each room, but when it comes to beauty, the Queen's Chamber takes the prize. The cobalt blue silk covering the walls (unfortunately now discoloured and torn in some parts) was handpicked by King Luís I to compliment the demanding tastes of his future wife, Italian princess Maria Pia.

Stroll Through the Majestic Jardim Botânico da Ajuda   GARDENS

MAP: **6** P84 **D1**

If you visit in the morning, you might have **Jardim Botânico da Ajuda** *(isa.ulisboa.pt; adult/child €2/1)* all to yourself, save for the gardeners, maintenance staff and the two resident white peacocks. Once a teaching garden for the king's children, the top terrace (accessed via ramps instead of stairs) has a partially obstructed view over Belém, Rio Tejo and Ponte 25 de Abril.

The actual attractions, though, are several baroque fountains surrounded by manicured hedges on the lower terrace and leafy tall trees and stone benches on the upper terrace. Pop in for a quick visit on your way down from Palácio Nacional da Ajuda to the centre of Belém.

✸ 1940 PORTUGUESE WORLD EXHIBITION

Museu de Arte Popular, Padrão dos Descobrimentos and Jardim Botânico Tropical were constructed for the 1940s Portuguese World Exhibition, which took place at the peak of the Estado Novo dictatorship. To celebrate the 800th anniversary of Portugal, the regime organised a six-month vanity fair that covered an area of more than 500,000 sq metres in Belém. It was a show of political propaganda disguised as national pride. Regrettably, plenty of those now must-see monuments continue to convey a message of greatness with poor or nonexistent historical context.

Admire the Crown Jewels at Museu do Tesouro Real   MUSEUM

MAP: **7** P84 **E1**

No other setting would be as perfect to showcase the royal jewels as Palácio Nacional da Ajuda (p89). The back of the building was closed off, and the interior courtyard now leads to **Museu do Tesouro Real** (tesouroreal.pt; adult/child €10/7).

Even though Portugal's history stretches back more than 800 years, only jewels from two 19th-century reigns have survived. On the bright side, a small collection means more time to see each piece in detail. One of the most beautiful pieces on display is the 1868 diamond- and gold-starred tiara and necklace combo designed for Queen Maria Pia.

Check Out Contemporary Art   MUSEUM

MAP: **8** P84 **C3**

The 'new' contemporary art museum in Belém may have rebranded from Coleção Berardo to **Museu de Arte Contemporânea MAC/**

CCB (ccb.pt/macccb; adult/child €12/free), but the namesake collection remains one of the centrepieces, with the same notable works from the 20th century taking over the 2nd floor – at least for the time being while the legal conundrum between the entrepreneur's foundation and the Portuguese government remains unresolved.

Currently managed by the CCB Foundation, this contemporary art museum has a second permanent exhibition dedicated to 1960s art on the lower ground floor, curated with pieces from three new collections owned by the foundation. With the same ticket, museum-goers can visit Garagem Sul, a repurposed garage on the south side of the building that houses temporary exhibitions on architecture.

Find Traces of Folk Art at Museu de Arte Popular   MUSEUM

MAP: **9** P84 **C4**

In 1940, it was a pavilion at the Portuguese World Exhibition. In 1948, it was officially Museu do Povo (Museum of the People).

 MANUELINE ARCHITECTURE

Portuguese Late Gothic style became known as Manueline after Dom Manuel I, the ruling king at the time (1495–1521). Inspired by Portugal's maritime expansion and the lands reached by sailors during that so-called Age of Discovery, the decoration of churches and monasteries incorporated sea elements, such as shells, anchors, ropes, seaweed and navigational instruments. Belém has a large concentration of these ornate and exuberant monuments, built to show power, superiority and the extent of the Portuguese empire through overseas aesthetic choices, such as the lace-style decorations found in temples in India.

Then, most likely because of its roots as a propaganda museum for the Estado Novo dictatorship, it closed permanently for decades until it reopened in 2016 under the name **Museu de Arte Popular** (*museusemonumentos.pt, adult/child €5/free*).

The exhibitions have shifted from a diverse array of folk art, traditional clothes and tools from mid-20th-century rural Portugal to a permanent showcase of Portuguese basketry and temporary six-month exhibitions that usually mix contemporary and folk art. The current shows won't appeal to everyone, but the frescoes depicting core values and honourable work (as imposed by the dictatorship then) in the main room are worth a look.

Ride to NOS Alive FESTIVAL

MAP: ⑩ P84 **A4**

NOS Alive (*nosalive.com*) is the goldilocks of city summer music festivals: far from the city centre but close enough to travel by train or tram back to Lisbon after the concerts. It's technically in Algés, but the train from Belém arrives there in less than five minutes.

Every year, NOS Alive boasts about having the best lineup, and the three-day festival in mid-July typically attracts an eclectic setlist, with established indie bands, new pop and hip-hop artists, and emergent Portuguese musicians. The big headliners are usually bands whose music has crossed generations, such as Pearl Jam, Arcade Fire, Radiohead and Arctic Monkeys.

Watch a Performance at Centro Cultural de Belém ARTS CENTRE

MAP: ⑪ P84 **C4**

With a calendar full of eclectic cultural events, including theatre, performance arts and music, it's not hard to find a performance at **Centro Cultural de Belém** (*ccb.pt*) that appeals. The cultural centre's strongest focus – and the concerts it was most popular for – had been jazz and classical music since it opened, but since 2024, more music genres have found a stage at CCB, such as the four-day mixed-genre festival Belém Soundcheck in March. Despite the changes, the New Year's Day orchestra concerts on 1 January remain a top event.

Understand Lisbon's Greatest Tragedy at Quake MUSEUM

MAP: ⑫ P84 **E3**

Although the Great Earthquake and its effects are discussed at length at many of the city's sights, **Quake** (*lisbonquake.com; adult/child €29/21*) quite literally shakes things up.

Each group of no more than 19 people is led through a series of rooms with interactive exhibitions on Earth's seismic activity and small-scale recreations until the main attraction: the 1755 Great Earthquake simulator. For those who might be triggered by quakes, head to the stationary pew at the back of the replicated church, where you can see the chain of events without having to be in the middle of it. This experience isn't available for children six and under.

Book your tickets in advance and arrive at least 10 minutes before your allotted time.

Wander Among Carriages at Museu Nacional dos Coches
MUSEUM

MAP: **13** P84 **E3**

In a neighbourhood known for its royal palaces, **Museu Nacional dos Coches** (*museudoscoches.gov. pt; adult/child €8/free*) is a popular must-visit for its repository of carriages that spans three centuries, most of them previously owned by the royal family. The museum's open space allows visitors to walk around each of the vehicles. Expect to spend at least an hour getting a closer look at all the details.

One of the most notable vehicles here is the landau in which the last king and his heir-apparent were assassinated by anti-monarchists

in 1908, two years before the First Portuguese Republic. The bullet holes on the door are easy to spot.

Enjoy the Frescoes at Antigo Picadeiro Real
MUSEUM

MAP: **14** P84 **D3**

Near Museu Nacional dos Coches, **Antigo Picadeiro Real** (*museuse monumentos.pt/en/museus-e-mon umentos/picadeiro-real; adult/child €5/free*) housed the coach museum until the collection outgrew the space. The collection here is now much smaller, but it's worth visiting the old royal riding arena. Start from the royals' portraits in the top-floor gallery, where you can also get a closer look at the ceiling frescoes.

On the ground floor, besides the dozen or so carriages, is a collection of uniforms, tools and weapons. It's believed the arena was used as a training battlefield for the royal army, which trained in front of an audience under the ruse of performing 'war games', a clever way not to spread panic about upcoming wars. Staff gladly share these and other stories about the place's history if you ask.

 LISBOA CARD

The most-visited monuments in Belém are free or have a reduced ticket price with the **Lisboa Card** (*shop.visitlisboa.com; 24-hour card adult/child €27/18*). It also includes free rides on all public transit networks that you can use to travel to and from the neighbourhood: train, bus and tram. This side of Lisbon has a higher concentration of must-sees, so the card is useful here. Despite what some outdated unofficial websites claim, card holders can't skip the line at all popular museums and monuments, including Mosteiro dos Jerónimos and Torre de Belém.

Explore MAAT's Art Spaces

MUSEUM

Shaped like a wave and covered in white, light-reflecting tiles, **MAAT** (*maat.pt; adult/child €11/free*) practically blends in with the riverbank, and its free-access terrace attracts the curious for different views of Rio Tejo.

Each space speaks to diverse audiences and interests. **MAAT Gallery** (MAP: ⑮ P84 E3) showcases works by known contemporary artists, which rotate every six months. Large-scale and often interactive art installations are on the main floor, while two smaller rooms have other showcases.

Next door inside a former power station, **MAAT Central** (MAP: ⑯ P84 E3) has a permanent exhibition dedicated to electricity (family-friendly guided tours are available on weekends), as well as Cinzeiro 8, a space for experimental and emergent artists invited by the gallery's curators.

Open 24 hours, **MAAT Garden** (MAP: ⑰ P84 E3) frequently stages performance art events.

Indulge in Pastéis de Belém

PASTRIES

MAP: ⑱ P84 D3

Unless you arrive at opening time (8am), **Pastéis de Belém** always seems to have a queue, but its crunchy, creamy, eat-in-one-bite custard tarts are worth the wait.

Although the gorgeous blue and white tiled walls encourage a longer stay, noisy patrons might break your concentration as you decide the right amount of cinnamon to sprinkle on your freshly baked *pastel de nata*. This culinary experience demands your full attention, so get a six-pastry pack to go (complimentary packets of sugar and cinnamon included) and eat them elsewhere before they're cold. Jardim Vasco da Gama across the street is a good spot for an impromptu picnic.

 PASTÉIS DE BELÉM VS PASTÉIS DE NATA

Are *pastéis de Belém* and *pastéis de nata* the same thing? They are both custard tarts, but only the ones made in Antiga Confeitaria de Belém can be called pastéis de Belém. The bakery has held the original secret recipe since its creation in 1837 by monks at Mosteiro dos Jerónimos. Countless versions of the pastry have popped up since then, though the differences are sometimes too subtle to notice. Now, there's hardly a single cafe or *pastelaria* (pastry and cake shop) in Portugal that doesn't sell custard tarts. Some clients are loyal to the originals, while others prefer the more buttery and flaky pastry at Manteigaria. Most don't mind as long as they're freshly baked.

EXPLORE

BELÉM

Best Places for...

 Budget   Midrange   Top End

See p84 for map of locations

Eating

Traditional Portuguese

Portugália
19 C4

A Lisbon classic in the middle of a riverside lake. Known for its steaks, this restaurant also serves seafood dishes. *noon-midnight*

O Prado
20 E3

Tables are covered in paper towels for faster service, and meals come in stainless steel platters. No frills, just food. *9am-midnight Tue-Sat, to 5pm Sun*

Breakfast & Brunch

MAAT Cafe & Kitchen
21 E3

This laid-back museum restaurant is a top spot for weekend brunch. *mercantina.pt/restaurantes/maat-cafe-kitchen; 11am-6.30pm Mon-Fri, from 10am Sat & Sun*

Augusto Lisboa
22 D3

All-day brunch with house-made ingredients and locally sourced sustainable products. We recommend the Portuguese Scrambled: eggs, mushrooms, cheese and grilled chorizo. *instagram.com/augustolisboapt; 9am-4.30pm Mon, Tue, Thu & Fri, to 5pm Sat & Sun*

Único
23 C4

This organic and sustainable restaurant inside Centro Cultural de Belém (p91) serves brunch all day with views of the river included. Gluten-free options are available. *instagram.com/unico_ccb; 9am-6pm Mon-Fri, from 10am Sat & Sun*

Pastries

Pastelaria Versailles
24 D3

The perfect *pastelaria* for a quiet breakfast before the crowds arrive and start hitting the major sights. *grupoversailles.pt; 8am-7pm*

Pastelaria Restelo
25 A3

The locals vouch for this spot. Its croissants are the best in town and worth the detour from riverside Belém. *pastelariaocareca.pt; 8am-8pm Wed-Mon*

Confeitaria Nacional
26 B4

Praça da Figueira's historic *pastelaria* opened a second location in Belém, and the classic pastries come with river views. *confeitarianacional.com; 9am-8pm*

Manteigaria
27 D3

Without fearing the competition, these *pastel de nata* specialists opened a shop near Pastéis de Belém (p93). Perfect excuse for a taste test. *manteigaria.com; 8am-9pm*

Contemporary Cuisine

Darwin's Cafe
28 A4

The Champalimaud Foundation's Mediterranean restaurant, within walking distance from

Torre de Belém (p85), is famous for its gorgeous views. *darwincafe.com; 12.30pm-1am*

Canalha

29 F3

The restaurant from award-winning chef João Rodrigues mixes the homely environment of a traditional *tasca* (tavern) with a menu of reinterpreted Portuguese seasonal comfort foods. *canalha.pt; 12.30-11pm Tue-Sat*

Guelra

30 D3

At this ocean-to-table restaurant, the fish is as fresh as it gets in this area. The main dishes are catch-of-the-day and paired with Portuguese wines produced by the restaurant. *guelraott.com; noon-11pm*

Ice Cream

Santini

31 E3

This Cascais-based artisanal ice cream shop brought all its flavours (and the trademarked red stripes) to a spot near Museu Nacional dos Coches. Marabunta (cream and dark chocolate chips) remains a classic. *santini.pt; noon-10pm*

Gelato Davvero

32 C3

The ice cream shop at Centro Cultural de Belém (p91) serves Italian gelato the Roman way, with optional whipped cream on top. *instagram.com/gelatodavvero; noon-8pm Sun & Mon, to 9pm Tue-Sat*

Drinking

Wine

Wine with a View

33 B4

Spot the red-and-cream-coloured cart parked near Torre de Belém (p85) and have a laid-back wine tasting with the on-duty ambassador. *winewithaview.pt; 10am-5pm*

Adega Belém Urban Winery

34 E3

Winemakers Catarina and David opened this winery in a former car repair shop. Wine and tapas tours on Fridays and Saturdays. *adegabelem.com; 11am-4pm Thu, to 7.30pm Fri, 11am-1pm Sat*

Gastrobar 38° 41'

35 C4

This sleek but casual riverside bar at Altis Hotel pours classic cocktails and Portuguese wine by the glass. *altishotels.com; 11am-midnight*

Shopping

Art & Souvenirs

Toranja

36 D3

You can buy a t-shirt or a mug with a yellow tram anywhere, but at Toranja, local artists design each piece. And there's more than just trams. *toranja.com; 9am-9.30pm*

Centro Português de Serigrafia

37 C3

CPS promotes Portuguese serigraphy artists and has only one shop – here at Centro Cultural de Belém (p91). *cps.pt; 10am-7pm Tue-Sun*

Markets

Feira Jardim Vasco da Gama

38 C3

Every first and third Sunday, artisans and antique dealers set up shop at Jardim Vasco da Gama. Scavenge for treasures or find new art. *9am-7pm Apr-Sep, to 5pm Oct-Mar*

See p106
for eating,
drinking and
shopping
listings

Explore
Parque das Nações

Three decades ago, Lisbon expanded east because of the Expo '98 World's Fair, turning a former industrial wasteland into the neighbourhood now known as Parque das Nações. It brought an expanded metro line and a new train station, and contemporary flats, office spaces and business hotels grew around the urban park, making it an open-air museum of cutting-edge architecture. Although the patchy pavements and benches' flaking paint signal the park's unfortunate state of neglect in recent years, Lisbon's east side remains a family-favourite destination, in part thanks to the popularity of the city's largest aquarium.

Getting Around

Ⓜ Metro
Most visitors use public transit to reach the east side. A trip on the Red Line from São Sebastião to Oriente takes about 20 minutes.

🚆 Train
Taking the CP urban train from Santa Apolónia is the fastest traffic-free way to reach the neighbourhood, but trains don't depart as often outside of rush hour.

🚌 Bus
Carris buses 728 (stops at Oceanário) and 759 (stops at Gare do Oriente) connect Lisbon's downtown to Oriente. Expect a slow trip and crowded vehicles.

★

THE BEST

VIEWPOINT Torre Vasco da Gama (p104)

FOR KIDS Oceanário de Lisboa (p99)

SUSTAINABLE RESTAURANT Sea The Future (p106)

HANDS-ON MUSEUM Centro de Ciência Viva (p104)

RIVERSIDE STROLL Parque Ribeirinho do Oriente (p105)

Torre Vasco da Gama (p104)
GI CRISTOVAO PHOTOGRAPHY/SHUTTERSTOCK ©

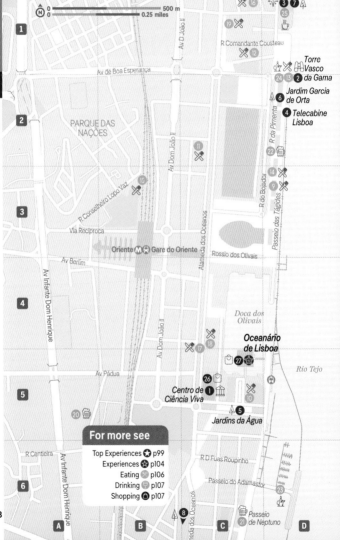

N
0 ———————— 500 m
0 ———————— 0.25 miles

R Comandante Cousteau

Av de Boa Esperança

Av de João II

PARQUE DAS NAÇÕES

Av Dom João II

R Conselheiro Lopo Vaz

Via Recíproca

Av Berlim

Oriente Ⓜ 🚆 Gare do Oriente

Alameda dos Oceanos

Rossio dos Olivais

Av Infante Dom Henrique

Av Dom João II

Av Pádua

Doca dos Olivais

Oceanário de Lisboa

Rio Tejo

Torre Vasco da Gama

Jardim Garcia de Orta

Telecabine Lisboa

R da Pimenta

Río Bojador

Passeio das Tágides

Centro de Ciência Viva

Jardins da Água

R Centieira

Av Infante Dom Henrique

R D Fuas Roupinho

Passeio do Adamastor

Alameda dos Oceanos

Passeio de Neptuno

For more see

⭐ **TOP EXPERIENCE**

Oceanário de Lisboa

For three decades, Oceanário de Lisboa has been Parque das Nações' most popular attraction – and not just for families with overexcited kids. Who wants to miss the opportunity to visit four different habitats and see dozens of marine species under one roof?

MAP P98, **C5**

Temporary Exhibitions

When visiting the **oceanário** *(oceanario.pt; adult/ child €25/15)*, before the main event, two opening acts are included with your ticket. These temporary exhibitions are usually art installations with a message of raising awareness for ocean preservation and sustainability. At the time of writing, Takashi Amano's Underwater Forests has taken over the first room, where it has been since 2015. It's designed to be a soothing, almost mesmerising experience, but unfortunately, the view is often obscured by passers-by who just want to see the fish up-close and skip ahead to what they really came for.

The second room has housed ONE since 2020, an immersive installation of underwater films made in Portugal by local artist Maya de Almeida Araújo.

Global Ocean

The central tank is ever present as you move from one habitat to the next and finally to the 'bottom of the ocean' on the lower level. You have plenty of opportunities to take a good look at all the fish and take photos of sharks, bull rays and funny-looking ocean sunfish.

PLANNING TIP
Buy tickets online in advance. When you arrive, there's a dedicated line for ticket holders. Plan for a morning visit and expect to tour the aquarium for at least an hour.

Scan QR code to purchase tickets.

Puffins & Penguins

The level of excitement that kids and grownups have when they first see the puffins and penguins is unparalleled. The birds, though, couldn't care less. In the next habitat – the Antarctic – the Magellanic penguins seem even more unfazed, and the only ones putting on a show are the Inca terns flying above gleeful visitors' heads.

Don't leave without learning the penguins' names (match the colour tags with the family tree on the info board), their lineage and history. Oceanário works hard to remind you that the animals aren't just there for show.

Sea Otters & Famous Fish

Over the last three decades, several generations of sea otters have delighted visitors, making these furry mammals the top attractions of the Pacific Ocean habitat. Spend some time here before heading to the fourth and final habitat. Seconds before you enter, you feel a puff of humid air, signalling that you've reached the Indian Ocean. Some kids take a quick look at the colourful fish and move along, but those aware of some of the residents' star quality squat near the water tanks to spot the blue tang and clownfish, the two species made famous in *Finding Nemo*.

Bottom of the Sea

On the lower level, visitors often skip through the rooms with the smaller aquariums not because of a lack of interest but because it's the last opportunity to spend time near the central tank. Kids sit on the carpeted floor as close to the glass as possible, while grownups try to grab a seat on the bench across from the tank. The space isn't exactly quiet (nowhere in Oceanário is), but the overall energy is calmer, perhaps because some exhaustion has started to sneak in by then.

ESCAPE THE CROWDS
The central aquarium can get busy and loud with visitors taking up every inch of free space, often tapping the glass in hopes the fish will look their way. (They can't see people on the other side.) If you feel overwhelmed or need a breather, find a bench in the less-crowded side wings.

DIOGO MENDES PINTO/SHUTTERSTOCK ©

It's a good time to remember the aquarium's educational purpose. In the small auditorium between rooms, watch the video (in Portuguese with English subtitles) about Oceanário and its mission. If you're pressed for time, the boards with information about each species highlight the effects of climate change on marine creatures on the brink of extinction and provide actionable tips for reducing your impact.

QUICK BREAK
Grab lunch at on-site **Restaurante Tejo**. The buffet-style restaurant has a varied Mediterranean cuisine menu, with plant-based and kid-friendly options.

🚶 WALKING TOUR

Walk Parque das Nações

Following the ocean theme of Expo '98, the public artworks and buildings in Parque das Nações designed for the event pay tribute to Portuguese navigators, life at sea and mythical marine creatures. Stroll amongst contemporary architecture and urban art created by renowned architects and artists.

START	END	LENGTH
Gare do Oriente	Jardim Garcia de Orta	2km; 1½ hours

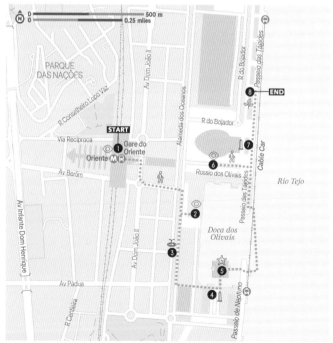

❶ Iconic Train Station

Designed by famed Spanish architect Santiago Calatrava, the iron and glass structure of **Gare do Oriente** is open to interpretation. Some say it's trees in a forest, while others see underwater plants. Look from across the street outside Vasco da Gama, and come up with your version.

❷ Gravity-Defying Roof

Designed by Portuguese architect Siza Vieira, the roof of **Pavilhão de Portugal** leaves visitors in as much awe now as it did 30 years ago when it was unveiled. The reinforced concrete structure appears as light as the sails it mimics.

❸ Cooling Eruptions

Along Alameda dos Oceanos, the six cone-shaped fountains of **Vulcões de Água** are covered in colourful *azulejos* (painted glazed tiles) and blast water every 25 seconds. On your way to the next stop, if the water is on, get your camera ready and wait for the next eruption.

❹ Sea Monsters

Outside Oceanário's entrance, slow down to see Pedro Proença's **Monstros Marinhos** made in *calçada portuguesa* (Portuguese cobblestone pavement). The Portuguese artist depicted these sea creatures as they are represented in medieval books.

❺ Aquatic Abode

Designed by US-based architecture firm Peter Chermayeff, **Oceanário de Lisboa** (p99) resembles an isolated concrete island. It's one of the neighbourhood's most recognisable buildings for its design and its work on ocean conservation and sustainability.

❻ Counting Flags

During the 1998 World Expo, the flags of the 146 countries that participated in the event lined the man-made lake at **Rossio dos Olivais**. In the intervening years, some flags have been removed, and others have been replaced, a testament to the ever-changing world where countries might cease to exist or make way for new ones.

❼ Bathing Muses

In the 1500s, Portuguese epic poet Camões created Tágides, the mythological nymphs that live in Rio Tejo. Four centuries later, Portuguese sculptor João Cutileiro gave them form when he made the marble statues at **Lago das Tágides**.

❽ Urban Botanical Garden

At riverside **Jardim Garcia de Orta**, sit in the shade of trees brought from other countries, take in the views and watch the cable cars crisscrossing the sky, with Torre Vasco da Gama and Ponte Vasco da Gama in the background.

EXPERIENCES

Have Fun Learning at Centro de Ciência Viva
MUSEUM

MAP: **1** P98 **C5**

At the interactive science museum **Centro de Ciência Viva** (pavcon hecimento.pt; adult/child €14/free), kids are encouraged to touch all displays. Temporary exhibitions take over the ground floor's open space and rotate every year or so.

Head to the Dòing room in the back to join a workshop where you can build robots, tools or electric circuit boards. If time is short, take the kids to the rooms on the 1st floor, where they can learn basic laws of physics (Explora), colour fish and then see them swimming in a virtual ocean (Fishanário), or blow off steam in various circus-inspired activities (Tcharan). Talk to one of the monitors to ride the flying bicycle, a fun way to test the laws of gravity 6m above the ground with peace of mind provided by a safety net. Before leaving, browse the list of Portuguese women in science on the digital display between Explora and Fishanário.

See East Lisbon from the Top of Torre Vasco da Gama
VIEWPOINT

MAP: **2** P98 **D1**

The lookout atop the 145m-high **Torre Vasco da Gama** (vascoda gamatower.com; adult/child €10/5) has the best views of East Lisbon. Walk around the glass dome, which gets a little warm on summer afternoons, and scan the QR codes on the window to learn more about the buildings in front of you, such as Ponte Vasco da Gama, Gare do Oriente and Oceanário.

Order a drink if you wish to stay longer, choose your favourite sight and have a seat (the couches are more comfortable than the tall chairs) to enjoy the view.

Party by the River at Rock in Rio
FESTIVAL

MAP: **3** P98 **D1**

For two weekends in June, **Rock in Rio** (rockinriolisboa.pt) trans-forms the north end of Parque Tejo into the City of Rock, a multistage venue with a free Ferris wheel, food stalls and lots of activities to

BEST TIME TO VISIT

For four months in 1998, all roads in Portugal led to the new Parque das Nações, as Expo '98 brought life to this once-neglected area. Even decades after the event, *lisboetas* (Lisbon residents) still see the urban park as a place to go. The park is alive during the day with tourists, families and workers from nearby offices, making this the best time to visit. However, after working hours, the place starts to feel a bit more 'abandoned', so you might feel a little uneasy in the riverside areas further from the Vasco da Gama shopping centre.

keep festival-goers busy between concerts. The Brazil-born music festival happens every other year (even-numbered years). Expect a diverse lineup for all generations of music fans, from trendy pop artists to classic rock bands.

Ride in Telecabine Lisboa
CABLE CAR

MAP: **4** P98 **D2**

Lisbon's only cable car system, **Telecabine Lisboa** (*telecabine lisboa.pt; round trip adult/child €9.50/6.50*) has been all the rage since it opened. It's a great way to cut short the 2km walk between Oceanário (p99) and Torre Vasco da Gama, especially on hotter days, but it's the opportunity to see all the famous contemporary buildings of Parque das Nações from above that attracts the crowds.

Each car has room for eight people, but if you're travelling alone and prefer to experience the short trip by yourself or if you're with a small group, the employees helping you hop on and off are usually accommodating. The cars might wobble slightly on breezy days, but the ride is smooth overall.

Walk Along Parque Ribeirinho do Oriente
PARK

MAP: **8** P98 **C6**

Parque Ribeirinho do Oriente, the east side's urban park, opened in 2020 and stretches for about 1km and connects Parque das Nações (Jardim do Neptuno) to

BEST GARDENS FOR KIDS

Jardins da Água

MAP: **5** P98 **C5**

This fun splash spot behind Oceanário is a balm on scorching summer days. Mind the stones across the lake, which get slippery fast. The water is about ankle deep.

Jardim Garcia de Orta

MAP: **6** P98 **D2**

In kids' vivid imaginations, this botanical garden (p103) can be a jungle with tall trees or an enchanted forest with wooden paths over streams. The enclosed garden is a great place to let older children run loose.

Jardins do Tejo

MAP: **7** P98 **D1**

This urban park resembles a series of small gardens stitched together. A favourite spot for kids is the playground at the north end.

Marvila (Doca do Poço do Bispo). Walk or cycle along the river (note that the first part of the path cuts through an industrial area but doesn't have much traffic), spotting pieces of urban art and stopping to see the view or grab a drink at one of the riverside cafes and kiosks. Opt for a morning visit, as this part of the city is still under development and might feel empty and unsafe after dark.

EXPLORE

PARQUE DAS NAÇÕES

Best Places for...

€ Budget   €€ Midrange   €€€ Top End

Eating

Family Meals

D'Bacalhau €€

9 D3

Salted cod (*bacalhau*) is unsurprisingly the star of this restaurant's menu, but it also serves vegetarian dishes. The kids' menu includes burgers, fish sticks and mini *bacalhau à Brás* (shredded cod with onions, eggs and potatoes). *restaurante bacalhau.com; noon-4pm & 7-11pm*

Sea The Future €

10 C5

This restaurant at Oceanário (p99) serves seasonal dishes (including plant-based options) made with local ingredients to reduce its carbon footprint. Pair your meal with organic coffee or a vegan Ocean Beer. *gruposushicafe.pt/ sea-the-future; 10am-7pm*

Breakfast & Brunch

Portela Cafés €

11 C2

Family-owned coffee shop chain with the vibe of a neighbourhood cafe. The aroma of just-brewed coffee is alluring. Order the Portela combo for a Portuguese-style breakfast experience. *portelacafes.pt; 7am-8pm Mon-Fri, 8am-7pm Sat & Sun*

A Taça Café €

12 C1

At this fusion brunch restaurant by the river, fixed menus mix the best of western and Moroccan cuisine. Reservations recommended. *8.30am-2.30pm Sun, Tue & Wed, to 7pm Thu-Sat*

Portuguese

Fifty Seconds €€€

13 D2

Small restaurant with one Michelin star at the top of Torre Vasco da Gama (p104). Chef Rui Silvestre's three tasting menus reflect his Portuguese, Mozambican and Indian roots. *fiftysecondsexperience.com; 7-9pm Tue-Sat*

See p98 for map of locations

Cantinho do Avillez €€

14 D3

Fusion restaurant from chef José Avillez that's reinventing traditional Portuguese dishes with international ingredients. Serves an all-inclusive menu (starter, main, drink, dessert and coffee) at lunch. *cantinhodoavillez. pt; 12.30-3pm & 7-11pm Mon-Fri, 12.30-11pm Sat, to 10pm Sun*

Casa Bota Feijão €€

15 B3

Locals flock here for the speciality *leitão à Bairrada* (spit-roast suckling pig) and don't bother to ask for a menu. Reservations recommended. *noon-3pm Mon-Fri*

Abacalhoar €€

16 C1

Cod is king at this small restaurant away from the neighbourhood centre. The menu has other food options, including a couple of vegetarian dishes. *facebook.com/ RestauranteAbacalhoar; noon-11pm Tue-Sat, to 5pm Sun*

Burgers & Pizza

Honorato Rio
 C4

Well-established local chain of restaurants specialising in artisanal burgers, with plant-based options available. *honorato.pt; noon-midnight*

ZeroZero
18 C4

Plenty of pizzas, from classic margherita to seasonal specialities with figs and ham, and plant-based versions, at this riverside spot. Kids get a special menu with a pasta dish or a small pizza. *pizzeriazerozero.pt; noon-midnight*

Luzzo
19 C1

This chain makes Roman and Neapolitan-style pizzas, with vegetarian options and a special menu for children. *pizzarialuzzo.pt; noon-3pm & 7-10.30pm Mon-Thu, noon-10.30pm Fri-Sun*

Drinking

Craft Beer

Fábrica Oitava Colina
20 A5

Head to one of Lisbon's oldest craft beer breweries, a short walk from Cabo Ruivo metro station, to taste new draughts or all-time favourite Urraca. *oitavacolina.pt; 5-10pm Wed & Thu, to 11pm Fri*

Sailors Bar
21 C6

Casual bar with river views, outdoor seating, and a good selection of national and international bottled craft beers. Drinkers who don't love beer can opt for classic cocktails. *instagram.com/sailors_bar; 3pm-2am Tue-Sat, to midnight Sun*

Irish & Co
22 D2

Lively pub with an Irish soul and a *lisboeta* heart. Good for nights when all you want is a cold pint with a view. *irishco.pt; noon-2am Sun-Thu, to 3am Fri & Sat*

Drinks with a View

Bliss Bar
23 D6

This casual bar near the marina has an outdoor terrace perfect for warm evenings. Pair your cold beer or refreshing cocktail with *petiscos* (tapas). *instagram.com/blissbarexpo; 2pm-2am*

Babylon 360°
24 D1

At the rooftop bar at Torre Vasco da Gama (p104), views come with spice-inspired cocktails and DJ sets. The dress code is casual chic (no flip-flops). *vascodagamatower.com; 6pm-midnight Sun-Wed, to 2am Thu-Sat*

Esplanando
25 D1

This pet-friendly cafe by the river with occasional cultural events serves only 100% Portuguese products. It's a popular spot for drinks and snacks with a view. *esplanando.com; noon-7.30pm Mon-Fri, from 9am Sat & Sun*

Shopping

Toys

Loja do Centro de Ciência Viva
26 C5

Wide selection of educational toys and books for kids at Centro de Ciência Viva's store. *loja.pavconhecimento.pt; 10am-6pm Mon-Fri, to 7pm Sat & Sun*

Oceanário de Lisboa Store
27 C5

Bright and colourful plush toys, clothes and tote bags produced sustainably line the shelves at the aquarium's official store. *oceanario.pt; 10am-8pm*

🚶 WALKING TOUR

Walk Beato to Marvila

On this walk, you'll see the future of Lisbon. When the historic centre became too expensive, hipsters headed east, and Beato and Marvila turned edgy, creative and innovative. Marvila became a hot spot for art galleries, craft beer taprooms and stylishly renovated warehouses, while Beato became a land of tech.

START	END	LENGTH
Hub Criativo do Beato	Fábrica de Braço de Prata	2km; 1 hour

1 Unicorn Factory

Start your walk from the **Beato Innovation District**, a place full of promise for Lisbon's future ever since the Portuguese capital became the home of Web Summit, an annual high-profile tech event. Grab a light lunch at A Praça, the on-site cafe, wine bar, bakery and organic produce market.

2 Dinner & A Show

Nothing is predictable in this part of town, and people who come here expect the unexpected. Take a slight detour to see **Palácio do Grilo**, a 300-year-old former private palace turned restaurant and events venue, where there's no such thing as a quiet dinner. Everything is an experience, and customers are part of the show.

3 Art & Craft Beer

After a long stretch of industrial streets lined with cheap traditional restaurants catering to workers on their lunch breaks, turn left on Rua José Domingos Barreiros and then right on Rua Capitão Leitão. This block between Beato and Marvila has no shortage of contemporary art galleries, craft beer taprooms and breweries, very on-brand for the neighbourhood. Stop at **Dois Corvos Taproom** for one of its craft beers on tap.

4 Sugar Street

Take a walk around the block and return to Rua do Açúcar. Most of Lisbon's 19th-century industries were established here, and the street name comes from an old sugar factory. The former warehouses are now cafes and restaurants. One at the end of the street houses the interactive museum **Ah Amália**, dedicated to Portugal's most famous *fadista* (fado singer).

5 Filming Location

Marvila's most famous warehouse is a movie star. The building with the art nouveau façade was a pharmacy in *Night Train to Lisbon*. It's now part of **8 Marvila**, the neighbourhood's trendiest cultural centre, shopping spot and food court.

6 First Cultural Hub

Fábrica de Braço de Prata is the last stop on this walking tour, but it's a return to the beginning of Marvila's artistic renaissance. It was established as an independent and alternative cultural hub, open to all and not too concerned with making money. The old ammunition factory keeps a regular calendar of concerts, exhibitions and workshops.

See p123
for eating,
drinking and
shopping
listings

Explore
Marquês de Pombal, Rato & Saldanha

The pedestrian-only lanes in the middle of tree-lined Avenida da Liberdade have been an invitation for slow strolls since the late 1800s. It's now a place to admire art nouveau buildings, high-end boutiques and old theatres. At the end of the 19th century, Lisbon expanded north of Marquês de Pombal, and Avenidas Novas (Saldanha and beyond) has carefully planned streets and apartment buildings, with squares, gardens and plenty of public transit options for optimal neighbourhood life. Mobility here is the best in Lisbon. To the west, Rato is a jumble of high-traffic streets with a handful of quiet places to breathe.

Getting Around

Ⓜ Metro
Metro is the fastest way to get around. The neighbourhood's main stations are Rato (Yellow Line), Marquês de Pombal (Yellow and Blue Lines), São Sebastião (Red and Blue Lines) and Saldanha (Yellow and Red Lines).

🚶 Walking
It's easy to get around the mostly flat ground of Marquês de Pombal and Saldanha on foot. Walking to Rato is possible, but it's uphill.

🚲 Bicycle
Saldanha has some of Lisbon's best cycling paths. Rent a Gira bike for up to 45 minutes (€2).

★ THE BEST

MUSEUM Centro de Arte Moderna (p114)

VIEWPOINT Jardim Amália Rodrigues (p119)

CULTURAL EVENTS Jardins do Bombarda (p118)

GARDEN Jardim Botânico de Lisboa (p121)

MODERNIST ARCHITECTURE Igreja de Nossa Senhora do Rosário de Fátima (p119)

Marquês de Pombal
DISHEV/SHUTTERSTOCK ©

Entre Campos 6

Entrecampos Metro Station

Campo Pequeno Metro Station 7

Igreja de Nossa Senhora do Rosário de Fátima 13

SALDANHA

Saldanha 10

Casa-Museu Dr Anastácio Gonçalves 21

Av da República

Cinema Nimas 24

Saldanha Metro Station

Museu Calouste Gulbenkian – Coleção do Fundador

Fundação Calouste Gulbenkian

Jardim Gulbenkian

Centro de Arte Moderna 32

São Sebastião Metro Station 5

Praça de Espanha Metro Station 6 3

For more see

Top Experiences ⭐ p114
Experiences 🎯 p118
Eating 🍽 p123
Drinking 🍷 p123
Shopping 🛍 p123

33

CAMPOLIDE

R de Campolide

Av Duarte Pacheco

Aqueduto das Águas Livres ⑪

R Marquês da Fronteira

Linha d'Água ⑮

Jardim Amália Rodrigues ⑭

Estufas ⑱

Alameda Edgar Cardoso

R Castilho

R Rodrigo da Fonseca

R Artilharia 1

Parque Eduardo VII ⑰

Alameda Cardeal Cerejeira

R Pascoal de Melo

R Dona Estefânia

R Jacinta Marto

R Gomes Freire

Jardins do Bombarda ②

R Luciano Cordeiro

R de São Lázaro

Campo dos Mártires da Pátria

Elevador da Lavra F

ESTEFÂNIA

Ⓜ Picoas
Ⓜ Picoas Metro Station ⑨

R Andrade Corvo

Av Duque de Loulé

R Tomás Ribeiro

R Viriato

Parque Metro Station ④

Parque Ⓜ

Av Sidónio Pais

Av Fontes Pereira de Melo

WC ①

Marquês de Pombal Metro Station ③

Marquês de Pombal Ⓜ

R Alexandre Herculano

R de Santa Marta

R Rodrigues Sampaio

R do Passadiço

R de São José

Av da Liberdade

Pç da Alegria

R do Salitre

Cinemateca Portuguesa ㉕

Praça ⑲
Dona Ajuda ⑳

Museu Nacional de História Natural ㉓

Jardim Botânico de Lisboa ㉒

Rato Ⓜ

R da Escola Politécnica

R de São Bento

Fundação Arpad Szenes-Vieira da Silva ⑯

Pç das Amoreiras

Reservatório da Mãe d'Água ⑫

R São Felipe Nery

R das Amoreiras

R do Sol ao Rato

R Dom João V

Av Pedro Álvares Cabral

R Saraiva de Carvalho

R Correia Teles

500 m
0.25 miles

113

Fundação Calouste Gulbenkian

Fundação Calouste Gulbenkian is a cultural hub and urban park that *lisboetas* (Lisbon residents) hold dear. The foundation is also popular for its two museums, which hold Portugal's most important art collections from the namesake Armenian-born founder.

MAP P112, **C3**

PLANNING TIP
Expect to spend half a day at the foundation. Weekday mornings are the quietest. Water bottles are no longer allowed after incidents with climate activists. Leave your belongings in the free cloakroom.

Scan this QR code for Museu Calouste Gulbenkian's audio guide.

Masterpieces Spanning 5000 Years

The private art collection of the **foundation** (*gulbenkian.pt*) is housed in **Museu Calouste Gulbenkian**, and a thorough visit can take a couple of hours. Most visitors glide through the first two sections (Egyptian Art and Greco-Roman Art), which have fewer pieces than the rest of the museum. Next, the intricate tapestries and ceramics from the Islamic East, Armenian and Far East art collections capture more attention.

The large section dedicated to European art is where most lose track of time, rush to photograph masterpieces by artists like Rubens and Degas (rooms 6 and 10), or simply stand close enough to see the brush strokes and admire the glimmering jewellery designed by René Lalique (room 11).

Contemporary & Modern Art Collection

The floor-to-ceiling glass wall in the lobby of the renovated **Centro de Arte Moderna** gives a warm welcome to visitors even before you step inside. That was the goal of architect Kengo Kuma and landscape designer Vladimir Djurovic, as the museum merges with the South Garden.

The main gallery, Galeria da Coleção, houses rotating exhibitions of the CAM permanent collection, which has nearly 12,000 artworks. Smaller rooms like Espaço Projeto and Sala de Som are re-

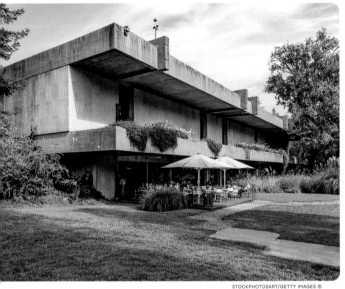

STOCKPHOTOSART/GETTY IMAGES ©

served for experimental art, temporary exhibitions and performance art.

Garden Relaxation

Jardim Gulbenkian offers a cool summer breeze and a surprisingly cosy atmosphere in the colder weather. It is mainly frequented by families and students on break from class at the nearby universities. Bring a book or a picnic and relax in the company of the resident birds (but don't feed the ducks, no matter how much they pester you).

When landscape architects Gonçalo Ribeiro Telles and António Viana Barreto designed the gardens the intention was to build a green refuge in the city, with a seemingly unplanned diversity of plants and trees, to be enjoyed by humans and the birds that choose this as their home.

QUICK BREAK
Head to
**Restaurante
Ice Gourmet**
between
museums for a
scoop of artisanal
ice cream or a
coffee. Grab
one of the red
armchairs by
the window
for chilled-out
garden views.

🚶 WALKING TOUR

Walk Marquês de Pombal

Home to planned parks, manicured gardens, museums, urban art, luxury shops and old theatres, this neighbourhood has a posh but artsy edge. On this walk, discover surprises, pieces of Lisbon's modern history, and the stories behind architectural details and the artists who have shaped the city.

START	END	LENGTH
Parque Gonçalo Ribeiro Telles	Praça da Alegria	3.5km; 1½ hours

1 Green Makeover

The final project by landscape architect Gonçalo Ribeiro Telles (1922–2020) was transforming a grimy car park and bus terminal into **Parque Gonçalo Ribeiro Telles**, with bike lanes, playgrounds and sprawling lawns.

2 Posh Heart

Enjoy the gardens at Fundação Calouste Gulbenkian (p114) before heading to **Avenida António Augusto de Aguiar**, a street where you'll spot the architecture design approved by the Estado Novo (Portugal's conservative dictatorship in power from 1933 to 1974) known as Português Suave (p120): straight lines, terracotta roofs, and wrought-iron balconies and doors.

3 Metro Art

Keil do Amaral (1910–75) designed **Parque Metro Station**, and modernist artist Maria Keil (1914–2012) decorated the interior with tile panels. Before the ticket validation machines, look for her signature geometric patterns. Her design choice influenced the future aesthetics of Lisbon's underground, and now every station features work from Portuguese artists.

4 Urban Park

Walk up to **Parque Eduardo VII**, an urban park of manicured lawns and paths paved with *calçada portuguesa* (Portuguese cobblestone pavement). Avenida da Liberdade stretches south of here at the feet of the 1930s statue of Marquês de Pombal, the man responsible for rebuilding Lisbon after the 1755 earthquake.

5 Rich Boulevard

Walk down wide **Avenida da Liberdade**. Lined with luxury stores and expensive restaurants, it's Lisbon's most expensive street. The 1950s **Cinema São Jorge** is a memory of a time when *lisboetas* dressed up for the movies.

6 Old Theatre District

During the Estado Novo era, censors combed through every film, play and book. Revue theatre managed to get away with a lot by using cleverly written musicals that were played at **Parque Mayer**. Today, this quarter is a kind of open-air museum, with working venue Cineteatro Capitólio.

7 Artists' Pavement

The pavement of Praça da Alegria bears the names of Portugal's greatest theatre professionals, old and new. **Passeio da Fama** is Lisbon's version of the Hollywood Walk of Fame, rendered in *calçada portuguesa* of course.

See Art at WC
ARTS CENTRE

MAP: **1** P112 **D6**

Art galleries often repurpose buildings or organise pop-up events in unusual locations, and the local government did just that with a disused underground public restroom near Marquês de Pombal, which became a cultural venue for art exhibits and occasional concerts.

The free-to-visit **WC** is a minuscule (but not too confining) art space under Jardim Camilo Castelo Branco, obviously without the facilities you'd see in a bathroom. Without a dedicated website, it's hard to keep track of the agenda, but check the advertising cube at the garden for events, which range from art shows to live concerts. Both emerging and established artists are invited to perform.

Discover Culture at Jardins do Bombarda
ARTS CENTRE

MAP: **2** P112 **F6**

Community-focused art project **Largo Residências** (*largoresiden cias.com*) took over the gardens of former mental health hospital Miguel Bombarda, which had been closed and practically abandoned since 2011. Simply called **Jardins do Bombarda**, this free cultural hub opened in 2024 with a slow start but a diverse calendar of events, including workshops, concerts and art shows.

The artistic complex has an art shop, cafe, restaurant and workrooms for creative residencies. The Jardins Românticos (romantic gardens) have wooden tables, benches, chairs and a communal vegetable garden at the back. A sign on the wall recommends visitors not use electronic devices to work in this space and simply enjoy nature.

Bazar Bombarda, a monthly market selling organic, sustainable and artisanal products, is one of the many community projects that found a home here.

Spot Metro Stations with Maria Keil's Tiles
PUBLIC ART

All metro stations in Lisbon are decorated with unique art, and the tiles are a sort of trademark. Visionary modernist painter Maria Keil (1914–2012) is responsible for that.

Keil's husband was the architect who designed the first stations when the Lisbon Metro opened in 1959. He refused to let the buildings' interiors be all cement and bare walls when confronted with budget cuts. It was Keil's idea to decorate the stations with *azulejos* (painted glazed tiles) against the critical voices telling her that working with such cheap material (at the time, tiles were primarily used in bathrooms) was beneath any serious artist.

She persisted and partnered with well-known tile company Viúva Lamego, designing the tile patterns in nine stations, most of them in this neighbourhood: the Blue Line's **Marquês de Pombal** (MAP: **3** P112 **D6**), **Parque** (MAP: **4** **D5**), **São**

Sebastião (MAP: **5** C4), and **Praça de Espanha** (MAP: **6** B3) and the Yellow Line's **Campo Pequeno** (MAP: **7** E2), **Entrecampos** (MAP: **8** D1), Picoas (MAP: **9** E5) and **Saldanha** (MAP: **10** E4). After her, every Lisbon Metro station featured work from prominent Portuguese artists.

Trace the History of Aqueduto das Águas Livres
ARCHITECTURE

The Campolide section of **Aqueduto das Águas Livres** (MAP: **11** P112 A6) is the most popular (partly because of the gruesome murders committed there by serial killer Diogo Alves in the late 1830s), but it's near **Reservatório da Mãe d'Água** (MAP: **12** P112 C7; *adult/child €4/free*) in Rato that you can stand near one of the arches and grasp the size of the massive construction. Decommissioned in 1968, the 18th-century arched structure carried drinking water to Lisbon's nearly 30 public fountains for almost two centuries.

Guided tours organised by **Museu da Água** (*facebook.com/museuagua; €18*) follow the water's old path through from Parque Florestal de Monsanto to Miradouro de São Pedro de Alcântara.

Check Out the Work of Portuguese Modernists at Igreja Nossa Senhora de Fátima
CHURCH

MAP: **13** P112 D3

Almada Negreiros (1893–1970) was a prolific and multigenre artist and the cofounder of the Portuguese modernism movement with Fernan-

do Pessoa. Much of Negreiros' work is scattered across Lisbon, mostly in museums and private collections, but one of the most surprising and lesser-known places to see his art is **Igreja de Nossa Senhora do Rosário de Fátima** (*paroquiansr fatima.com; free*), a 1938 Catholic church that features Negreiros' stained-glass windows and mosaics.

Enjoy the calming atmosphere surrounded by the works of some of the period's most accomplished artists, including Barata Feyo's Christ on the Cross. Be mindful of religious services when you visit.

Relax at Jardim Amália Rodrigues
GARDENS

Named after Portugal's most famous *fadista* (fado singer) and designed by Gonçalo Ribeiro Telles (one of the landscape architects who designed the award-winning gardens at Fundação Calouste Gulbenkian; p114), **Jardim Amália Rodrigues** (MAP: **14** P112 C5) has one of the neighbourhood's best views. To the north of Parque Eduardo VII, the garden's outdoor amphitheatre has open views over Avenida da Liberdade and Rio Tejo in the background.

As an environmentalist, Ribeiro Telles always considered the coexistence of humans and nature when designing a garden. The carefully selected plants and trees are endemic and accustomed to Portugal's climate. The human-made lake in the centre is a soothing water feature that attracts

Visit Vieira da Silva, a Museum Inside an Old Silk Factory   MUSEUM

MAP: 16 P112 C7

Away from the neighbourhood's main sights, **Fundação Arpad Szenes–Vieira da Silva** (*fasvs. pt; adult/child €7.50/free*) isn't the kind of place you stumble upon. Dedicated to the life and art of Lisbon-born Maria Helena Vieira da Silva and her husband, Arpad Szenes, the small museum is a short walk from Rato station. Before the station's ticket valida-tion gates, look for two tile panels opposite one another depicting a painting from each artist.

Vieira da Silva chose the old silk factory across from Jardim das Amoreiras to house a museum of her art. She wanted to maintain the space's bare walls and minimalism so that only the art would shine.

Stroll Down Parque Eduardo VII   PARK

MAP: 17 P112 D6

From the terrace-like viewpoint on the north end, look to see how the perfectly manicured lawn in the centre of **Parque Eduardo VII** contrasts with the side wings, which are full of trees and gentle slopes ideal for sitting with a book or soaking up the sun. The park stretches down and seems to fuse with Marquês de Pombal and Avenida da Liberdade all the way to Rio Tejo. Stroll down the lanes of *calçada portuguesa,* but be mindful of occasionally slippery and loose rocks.

Over the years, this urban park has become more popular as a venue for large events than as one of Lisbon's top gardens. **Feira do Livro de Lisboa** (Lisbon's Book Fair) gathers large and independ-ent publishers in June and attracts book lovers every year with author signings, book launches and concerts.

🏛 PORTUGUÊS SUAVE

The city expansion to Avenidas Novas in the 1930s followed the Estado Novo–sanctioned austere aesthetics, in which function was above form and the (subtle) embellishments made a political statement. The authoritarian regime called it 'truly Portuguese', but architects mocked the lack of creativity and called it 'Português Suave'. The name was an insult (meaning bland), but it stuck. The buildings look midcentury modern (straight lines, colourful walls), but the subtle traditionalist details are there. Terracotta shingles and weathervanes suggest the countryside, while wrought-iron features are reminiscent of the medieval era when Portugal became a country.

Wander Among a Sea of Green at Estufas
GARDENS

MAP: **18** P112 **C5**

The quiet green haven next to Parque Eduardo VII wasn't planned when it sprang up in the 19th century, but now it's inconceivable to think of Lisbon without **Estufas** (*estufafria.lisboa.pt; adult/child €3.50/free*). Get lost among every plant imaginable, sheltered from the busy city outside.

Choose your ideal setting: cool and breezy Estufa Fria, balmy and perfumed Estufa Quente or the smaller Estufa Doce (home of the succulents). Or don't pick a favourite and walk the gravel paths, climb the stairs and scan the QR codes for more details on plants that catch your eye. Plenty of benches are scattered around the gardens for short breaks.

Shop with Impact
VINTAGE

You never know what you might find at these two socially-minded stores, where every item for sale has been donated, and profits fund social projects and help local NGOs.

Praça (MAP: **19** P112 **C7**; *facebook.com/p.r.a.c.a.rato*), the larger shop inside the former Mercado do Rato, sells used furniture, books, magazines and postcards. It also has nooks dedicated to DVDs and VHS tapes, CDs and vinyl records, and used-but-loved toys. Next door, **Dona Ajuda** (MAP: **20** P112 **C7**; *donaajuda.pt*) sells mostly clothes and accessories.

Admire Casa-Museu Dr Anastácio Gonçalves
MUSEUM

MAP: **21** P112 **E4**

Impossible to miss, art nouveau **Casa Museu Dr Anastácio Gonçalves** (*bilheteira.museusemonumentos.pt; adult/child €5/free*) stands out among the more modern buildings of Saldanha. The early 1900s house, previously owned by Lisbon-based painter José Malhoa, is wonderfully preserved and has an impressive collection of furniture, decor pieces, and artworks by Malhoa, Columbano Bordalo Pinheiro and Silva Porto.

The staff efficiently provide guidance throughout the house, but their overzealousness can break the mood when you're lost in contemplation. Fortunately, they don't rush you out of a room, and if you strike up a conversation about a specific piece, they diligently share their knowledge.

Enjoy Quiet Time at Jardim Botânico de Lisboa
GARDENS

MAP: **22** P112 **D8**

Created as a botanical research garden in the 19th century for the University of Science next door (now Museu Nacional de História Natural), **Jardim Botânico de Lisboa** (*museus.ulisboa.pt; adult/child €5/free*) is home to more than 2000 species of exotic plants.

After the gate and the ticket office, once you start descending toward the amphitheatre at the heart of the garden, you'll find so much tranquillity that you almost forget the garden is surrounded by busy streets. Located between the neighbourhoods of Príncipe Real and Rato, it's a welcome refuge of tall trees and shade on warmer days. The kid-favourite butterfly house no longer exists, but it's been replaced with a *jardim dos sentidos* (sensory garden) with suggested activities, including a barefoot walking path.

Have Family Fun at Museu Nacional de História Natural   MUSEUM

MAP: **23** P112 **D8**

Home to skeletons, replicas of prehistoric birds and taxidermied animals, **Museu Nacional de História Natural** (*museus. ulisboa.pt; adult/child €6/free*) is a classic science museum. The 19th-century building is an attraction itself, particularly the chemistry lab and lecture room. If you're squeamish, skip the room of models showing the common symptoms of skin diseases – it's not a pretty sight.

Several exhibitions are marked as family friendly. Find a more

hands-on exhibition on the 1st floor (room 14), where visitors learn physics through simple experiences. Check the museum's website for a calendar of events.

Watch Classic & Avant-Garde Films at Independent Cinemas   CINEMA

Owned by Portuguese film producer Paulo Branco, **Cinema Nimas** (MAP: **24** P112 **E4**; *medeiafilmes.com*) is an institution. Focusing on curated programmes dedicated to a specific director or a genre, this one-room theatre in the basement of an apartment building is the place to go for classics you haven't seen on the big screen yet or in a long time.

Near Avenida da Liberdade, **Cinemateca Portuguesa** (MAP: **25** P112 **D8**; *cinemateca.pt*) is the country's largest repository of Portuguese films and organises monthly screenings of national and international movies. Summers are particularly popular because of **Cinema na Esplanada**, outdoor film viewings on the terrace of 39 Degraus.

 OVERCOMING CENSORSHIP AT CINEMA SÃO JORGE

In 1950, Portugal's largest cinema opened. During the Estado Novo dictatorship, censors (and sometimes dictator António Salazar himself, it seems) used the 21-seat cubicle-sized film screening room Sala Rank on the top floor, to pre-screen foreign films and decide what to censor 'for the good of the nation'. Today, **Cinema São Jorge** is the home of Lisbon's most influential independent film festivals, including IndieLisboa (May), Queer Lisboa (September) and MOTELX (September).

See p112 for map of locations

Best Places for...

G Budget **GG** Midrange **GGG** Top End

Eating

Cafes

Pastelaria Versailles G

26 E4

The fully stocked case at this classic *pastelaria* is heaven for those with a sweet tooth and torment for the undecided. *grupo versailles.pt; 7am-10pm*

Portuguese

Galeto GG

27 E4

A Lisbon institution, this open-late restaurant is popular for after-hours meals, whether you feel like breakfast at 2am or the comforts of chicken soup. *7.30am-3am*

É Um Restaurante GG

28 E8

A project by nonprofit CRESCER, this Mediterranean restaurant trains and employs people experiencing homelessness. *eumrestaurante.pt; 12.30-3pm & 7-10pm Wed-Sat*

Suzana G

29 D5

There is love behind each Portuguese dish with a contemporary twist without being pretentious. *instagram .com/suzana_restaurante; noon-3pm & 7-10pm Mon-Fri*

Drinking

Cocktails & Wine

Red Frog

30 E8

This reservations-only speakeasy bar near Avenida de Liberdade has an extensive cocktail menu. 'Press for Cocktails' to enter. *redfrog.pt; 6pm-1am Tue-Sat*

SEEN Sky Bar

31 D7

Hotel Tivoli Avenida's busy rooftop bar has one of the best views in the neighbourhood. Good selection of Portuguese wines by the glass. *skybarrooftop. com; 12.30pm-1am Sun-Thu, to 2am Fri & Sat*

Shopping

Books & Magazines

Under the Cover

32 D3

A curated selection of Portuguese and foreign independent magazines lines the walls of this small bookshop. *under thecover.pt; 11am-7pm Mon-Fri, noon-6pm Sat*

Bookshop Bivar

33 F4

This small family-owned shop sells only secondhand fiction and nonfiction books in English. *instagram.com/ bookshopbivar; 11am-6pm Tue-Sat*

For Kids

FuFu Loja Atelier

34 E7

Family-owned shop with books, toys and regular workshops for families. Home to the rag dolls Fulana Beltrana Sicrana, created by one of the owners. *fufu-lojaatelier. com; noon-7pm Tue-Fri, 11am-1pm & 2.30-5pm Sat*

See p137
for eating, drinking and shopping listings

Explore
Estrela, Lapa
& Alcântara

This area of Lisbon is a neighbourhood of contrasts. On the west side, markedly industrial and business-oriented Alcântara has used its iron and rust to its advantage, turning a bridge and an old factory into tourist attractions and old warehouses into bars, nightclubs, and restaurants. It also has a quiet space for walking or cycling by the river. To the north, tree-lined boulevards, small squares and romantic gardens define Lapa and Estrela. On the eastern edge are riverside nightlife hot spot Santos and Madragoa's jumble of narrow cobblestoned streets.

Getting Around

Tram
Take tram 18E or 15E from Cais do Sodré to Museu Nacional de Arte Antiga (Cais Rocha), Pilar 7 (Alcântara–Av 24 de Julho) and LX Factory (Calvário). Use 25E for Estrela.

Train
Use the train (departures every 30 minutes) to skirt traffic between Cais do Sodré and Museu do Oriente (Alcântara-Mar).

Bus
Buses 727 (from Rato to Restelo) and 67B (Estrela–Basílica) cover most of the neighbourhood and top attractions.

★
THE BEST

ART MUSEUM Museu Nacional de Arte Antiga (p128)

URBAN PARK Tapada das Necessidades (p135)

POST-INDUSTRIAL SITE LX Factory (p136)

MUSEUM FOR KIDS Museu da Marioneta (p134)

GARDEN Jardim da Estrela (p132)

LX Factory (p136)

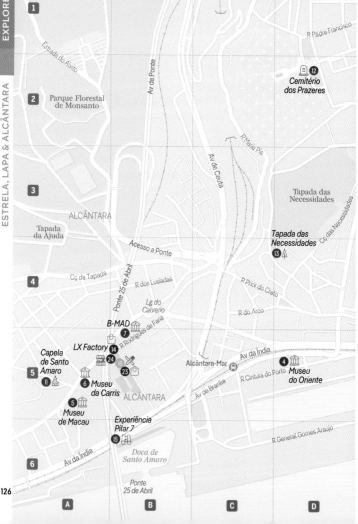

A

B

C

D

1

Estrada do Alvito

Parque Florestal
de Monsanto

2

Av da Ponte

R Padre Francisco

Cemitério
dos Prazeres 12

R Maria Pia

Av de Ceuta

Tapada das
Necessidades

3

ALCÂNTARA

Tapada
da Ajuda

Tapada das
Necessidades

Acesso a Ponte

Cç da Tapada

4

R dos Lusiadas

Ponte 25 de Abril

Lg do
Calvario

Tapada das Necessidades 13

R Prior do Crato

R do Arco

B-MAD 7

LX Factory 14

R Rodrigues de Faria

Alcântara-Mar

Av da Índia

R Cintura do Porto

Museu
do Oriente 4

24

Capela
de Santo
Amaro 11

23

Museu
da Carris 6

ALCÂNTARA

Av de Brasília

5

Museu
de Macau 5

Experiência
Pilar 7 15

Doca de
Santo Amaro

R General Gomes Araujo

6

Av da Índia

Ponte
25 de Abril

A

B

C

D

E · R. Almeida e Sousa

R. Coelho da Rocha

R. Saraiva de Carvalho

10 Casa Fernando Pessoa

Cemitério dos Ingleses

ESTRELA

Casa Museu de Amália Rodrigues 9

R. da Imprensa Nacional

1

Casa do Jardim da Estrela 2

Jardim da Estrela 1

R. de São Bernardo

R. de Santo Amaro

R. Saraiva Carvalho

R. do Patrocínio

Basílica da Estrela 3

Cç. da Estrela

R. de São Bento

R. de São Bento

2

R. de Borges Carneiro

R. de Santana à Lapa

R. da Lapa

R. do Quelhas

R. das Trinas

R. das Francezinhas

Av. Dom Carlos I

3

Av. Infante Santo

R. de São Caetano

R. das Praças

MADRAGOA

Museu da Marioneta 8

17

25

20

21

LAPA

R. de São Domingos

R. Garcia da Horta

R. da Esperança

22

Lg. de Santos

R. do Pau de Bandeira

R. Ribeiro Sanches

R. das Janelas Verdes

19

Cç. Ribeiro Santos

Av. 24 de Julho

Santos

SANTOS

4

R. Presidente Arriaga

R. do Olival

Av. de Brasília

Museu Nacional de Arte Antiga

Av. 24 de Julho

Doca de Alcântara

16

5

Rio Tejo

For more see

Top Experiences 🟢 p128
Experiences ⭐ p132
Eating 🔵 p137
Drinking 🟣 p137
Shopping 🔴 p137

6

N 0 ————————— 500 m
0 ————————— 0.25 miles

E F G H

Museu Nacional de Arte Antiga

The oldest art museum in the country, Museu Nacional de Arte Antiga has an impressive collection of European and Portuguese artworks, most considered masterpieces. Staff welcome art connoisseurs and fans with a warmth and enthusiasm that's rare in Lisbon museums.

MAP P126, **F4**

PLANNING TIP
You can easily spend a half day exploring the museum's four floors. Arrive in the morning so that you don't feel rushed.

Scan this QR code for information about temporary exhibitions.

Portuguese & European Masterpieces

The 12 rooms on Floor 3 of the **museum** (museude arteantiga.pt; adult/child €10/free) have enough Portuguese paintings and sculptures to keep visitors busy, but it's the ongoing art restoration work that draws the most attention. The process of returning the 15th-century *Painéis de São Vicente* to its original form has been complex. This section's other stars are Domingos Sequeira's *Coroação da Virgem* (1830) and *Adoração dos Magos* (1828), bright and almost ethereal interpretations of a religious theme that contrast with the heavy and sombre depictions elsewhere in the museum. *Inferno* (early 1500s) by an unknown artist is a good example of how pain can leap out of a painting.

The 14 rooms dedicated to European Paintings on Floor 1 will take up most of your time if you want to cover the whole floor thoroughly. One of the museum's most famous paintings is Hieronymus Bosch's Triptych of the *Temptation of St Anthony*.

Art from Portuguese 'Discoveries'

Portugal has yet to come to terms with the negative effects of its past as a colonising country. Many older museums still label collections from the 15th and 16th centuries as from the 'age of discoveries'

GREG ELMS/LONELY PLANET ©

and often present a one-sided historical perspective. However, at Museu Nacional de Arte Antiga, the pieces on display aren't indigenous artworks 'brought' from former colonies. Donated to the museum or purchased abroad, they mostly depict the cultural exchanges between the Portuguese and the local communities. But if you wish to skip this collection on floor 2 entirely, avoid rooms 14 to 18.

The Garden & New Acquisitions

On warm days, head to the interior garden for the views of the river and a coffee in the company of statues. Before leaving the museum, stop at the ground-floor lobby, where the museum proudly displays its latest purchases, some of them important Portuguese art pieces that almost ended up in private collections.

QUICK BREAK
Head to **Catch Me** for a Mediterranean lunch or drinks with a view of Rio Tejo while soaking up the sun.

WALKING TOUR

Walk Madragoa & Santos

The small districts of Madragoa and Santos don't have a huge number of monuments and museums because the place is the attraction here. Stroll through the quiet, narrow cobblestone streets of one of Lisbon's oldest quarters, Madragoa, and discover the artsy vibe of Santos' bars and restaurants.

ESTRELA, LAPA & ALCÂNTARA

START	END	LENGTH
Chafariz da Esperança	Jardim Nuno Álvares	1km; 1 hour

MADRAGOA

R do Quelhas
Tv do Pasteleiro
START 1
Av Dom Carlos I
R do Poço dos Negros
R do Garciás
2
R das Madres
4
C Marquês Abrantes
3
R da Esperança
Cç Marquês de Abrantes
R do Instituto Industrial
5
Lg de Santos
6
END 7
Cç Ribeiro Santos
Av 24 de Julho
R da Cintura do Porto de Lisboa
Santos Train Station
SANTOS
Rio Tejo

N
0 — 200 m
0 — 0.1 miles

EXPLORE

① Baroque Water Fountain

The 18th-century baroque water fountain **Chafariz da Esperança** marks the entrance to Madragoa. Go up Rua da Esperança and take the first right to Travessa do Pasteleiro, a steep side street leading into the heart of this historic quarter.

② Classic Street

Pedestrian-only **Rua das Madres** hits all the marks of a classic Lisbon neighbourhood: *calçada portuguesa* (Portuguese cobblestone pavement), laundry drying on clotheslines in windows, small houses with colourful trimmings and traditional restaurant Varina da Madragoa with homemade-style Portuguese meals.

③ Old Convent

Walk along quiet Rua das Madres and make a left at Calçada Castelo Picão. The corner building on your right is the former **Convento das Bernardas**, which now houses Museu da Marioneta, the puppetry museum that's a favourite among Lisbon families.

④ Neighbourhood Borderline

From the convent, turn left down Rua da Esperança. This street is a sort of border between Madragoa and Santos and is lined with cafes, restaurants and shops. Stop by **Parra Wine Bistro** for *petiscos* (tapas) paired with Portuguese wine.

⑤ Heart of Santos

Walk down Travessa dos Barbadinhos and turn left on Calçada Marquês de Abrantes. At the end of the street, walk around the corner on your right (mind the tram) to the heart of Santos and notice the change of atmosphere from quiet neighbourhood to bustling bars and cafes. Grab a pint at kiosk-turned-bar **Rudy Giuliani's Secret Bar**.

⑥ Neighbourhood Theatre

It's hard to miss the pale green art deco building that stands out from the rest. **Teatro A Barraca** is one of the oldest theatre companies in Lisbon, and it maintains a regular calendar of plays (in Portuguese).

⑦ Leafy Refuge

Jardim Nuno Álvares is a gated public garden at the neighbourhood's edge. Sit for a while and enjoy some quiet time (or not, if the playground is full of jolly kids).

Unwind at Jardim da Estrela

GARDENS

Jardim da Estrela (MAP: ❶ P126 **F1**), the 19th-century Romantic gated public garden across the street from Basílica da Estrela, is used by locals (sometimes as a shortcut between Estrela and São Bento) and tourists. It's an excellent place to read a book in the shade, take a break or have a drink at one of the kiosks-turned-cafes. It's not quiet and secluded, though, as it sits in the middle of a high-traffic zone, so expect constant urban noise on weekdays.

Casa do Jardim da Estrela (MAP: ❷ P126 **F1**; *instagram.com/casa dojardimdaestrela*), a free-to-visit cultural centre run by the city, puts on sustainability-focused cultural events. The main lobby has rotating temporary exhibitions.

Peek Inside Basílica da Estrela

CHURCH

MAP: ❸ P126 **F2**

You might see or hear baroque **Basílica da Estrela** before you arrive. Its dome is visible from afar, and the bell tolls every 15 minutes like, well, clockwork. The church is free to visit (mind the religious services), and attention-grabbing details and priceless features include the pink and blue marble covering the walls and the ceiling and the frescoes behind the main altar and side wings.

Visiting the roof costs €4, but after the steep climb on a narrow staircase (114 steps to be exact) you're rewarded with views over the Estrela neighbourhood.

Admire Asian Art

MUSEUM

Portugal's connection to Japan and China started with the second wave of sea explorations in the 16th century. Macau specifically became the long-lasting symbol of symbiosis between European and Asian cultures. These two museums in Lisbon entirely dedicated to Asian art continue to foster that relationship.

At **Museu do Oriente** (MAP: ❹ P126 **D5**; *foriente.pt; adult/child €8/2.50*), head to floor 1 for the Kwok On collection (Asian

---

 FUTURE METRO ROUTES

At the time of writing, Lisbon Metro's Green Line expansion was reaching its final stages, and the new Santos and Estrela stations are expected to open in late 2025. The much-anticipated subway connection will change the Green Line's layout, making it possible to travel from Cais do Sodré to Rato without switching lines thanks to new stops in the Madragoa neighbourhood (Santos station) and near Basílica da Estrela. The planned Red Line expansion (set to open in 2026) will add new stops in Campo de Ourique and Alcântara.

performance art and religion) and the 'Portuguese Presence in Asia' section, with artworks that blend Asian and Portuguese styles, including a must-see collection of Nanban art (Japanese art created after first contact with Portuguese).

Off the sightseeing route, the government-managed **Museu de Macau** (MAP: ❺ P126 A5; *cccm. gov.pt; adult/child €3/free, cash only*) highlights the relationship between Portugal and Macau, one of Portugal's former colonies. On the ground floor, see replicas of maps and documents for historical context, a small section dedicated to Chinese religions (with small statues of deities and shrines) and the mix of cultures once Christianity arrived.

Travel by Tram at Museu da Carris   MUSEUM

MAP: ❻ P126 A5

Public transportation company Carris has been part of Lisbon's history since it built the first funiculars and American-style trams in the late 19th century, and those funiculars and trams have become iconic images of the city.

The first section of **Museu da Carris** (*museu.carris.pt; adult/ child €4.50/free*) traces the company's timeline using documents, photos and old tickets. Then comes the treat of riding an old tram to the second and final section, a warehouse with buses and trams, old and new, on display.

Although the tram drivers don't mind answering questions and perhaps sharing personal anecdotes about their experience driving a tram through Lisbon's traffic, consider booking a guided tour, especially if you're travelling with kids.

Check Out B-MAD's Art Deco Collection   MUSEUM

MAP: ❼ P126 B4

A project from collector and entrepreneur Joe Berardo, **B-MAD** (*bmad.pt; adult/child €6/free*) houses his private collection of art deco and art nouveau furniture and art. Lisbon's first museum dedicated to these artistic styles is set in a restored 18th-century palace, and visitors stroll through each room, decorated with Tiffany stained-glass lamps and Picasso paintings, as if they were guests in someone's house.

Visits are guided and scheduled in advance. The one-hour tour doesn't leave much time to appreciate the details of all the pieces, especially with larger groups, as the guides, though cordial and knowledgeable, are eager to respect the timing.

The tour ends with a wine tasting (optional but included in the ticket price), provided by Berardo's Setúbal-based wine estate Bacalhôa. The tasting is paired with a sales pitch – if you feel inclined, grab a bottle of Moscatel wine from the museum's shop.

Take the Kids to Museu da Marioneta

MUSEUM

MAP: **8** P126 **G3**

Compact and cosy, **Museu da Marioneta** (*museudamarioneta. pt; adult/child €5/free*) at Convento das Bernardas is a favourite spot for Lisbon families. It keeps kids entertained on rainy mornings and scorching summer afternoons.

The collection is small but diverse and includes Asian and African masks, Punch and Judy and Sicilian puppets, and theatre props. It also dedicates an exhibition to Bonecos de Santo Aleixo, traditional Portuguese-made marionettes that have been crafted in the southern region of Alentejo since the 18th century.

The museum is also the headquarters of **FIMFA**, Lisbon's international puppet theatre festival. This annual event travels around the city every May with puppet shows and performances in several venues.

Walk Through the House of Fado Diva Amália Rodrigues

MUSEUM

MAP: **9** P126 **H1**

Casa Museu de Amália Rodrigues (*amaliarodrigues.pt; adult/child €7/free*), the last home of Portugal's most famous fado diva, is a repository of moments from her career and life. Her achievements and personality shine through in every corner of her home, from her decor choices and personal belongings to painted portraits and the collection of dresses, shoes (of which you see only a small fraction) and the flashy jewels she wore on stage.

If he's in the mood for a chat, visitors get to interact with someone who knew her well: Chico, her pet parrot. Tours are all guided, and time slots are adhered to. Live fado concerts take place in the garden on Thursdays, Fridays and Sundays at 6pm.

Visit Casa Fernando Pessoa, the Poet's Last Home

MUSEUM

MAP: **10** P126 **F1**

Casa Fernando Pessoa (*casa fernandopessoa.pt; guided tour €6; self-guided visits adult/child €5/ free*), the last official address of the famous modernist and Lisbon-born writer, is a rare window into his life and his complex and still not thoroughly studied work. Book a guided tour to let a Pessoa expert lead you from the ground floor to his bedroom on the 1st floor, where the tour ends, sometimes later than the scheduled hour.

If you are intrigued by the author's work, browse the on-site free-access library and leaf through the pages of every known published and translated book by and about Fernando Pessoa.

Find the Unexpected at Capela de Santo Amaro

CHURCH

MAP: **11** P126 **A5**

In Lisbon, climbing a seemingly never-ending staircase or walking up a steep hill almost always pays off. **Capela de Santo Amaro** is a trek worth the reward.

This off-the-beaten-path 16th-century church looks out of place in a markedly industrial neighbourhood like Alcântara. Visitors come for the views, which aren't too shabby but miss some of the wow factor, but the real prize is the building itself, with its unusual round shape. Baroque tile panels cover the lobby walls behind wrought-iron gates. If you're fortunate enough to find it open (the official schedule is 11am to 5.30pm Tuesday to Sunday, but hours vary), don't miss the opportunity to step inside the hall.

Wander Through Cemitério dos Prazeres CEMETERY

MAP: **12** P126 **D2**

The last stop on trams 28E and 25E, **Cemitério dos Prazeres** is a magnificent example of late 19th-century funeral architecture, with tall cypress trees, wide lanes and elaborate mausoleums. The cemetery is the final resting place of several Portuguese musicians, actors, writers and politicians, and at the Artists' Plot, you'll find one of the best views of Ponte 25 de Abril.

Inside the small chapel, visit the room where doctors performed autopsies before there were morgues. To show respect for the loved ones of the deceased, they did autopsies at the cemetery before the funeral rites.

Enjoy the Quiet at Tapada das Necessidades PARK

MAP: **13** P126 **D4**

Tapada das Necessidades isn't what you'd call a secret, but perhaps you'll notice locals using it more than tourists. The gated dog-friendly park has a few resident ducks, geese and peacocks, and you'll find lakes and lots of nooks and areas to explore. The south entrance, closest to Alcântara, has longer opening hours (8am to 8pm April to September, to 6pm October to March). The north

---

 MOCAMBO TO MADRAGOA

No signs reveal Madragoa's 16th-century name: Mocambo, the word for a small village in Umbundu, one of the languages spoken in Angola. Enslaved Africans were allowed to live in this area, have a home address (but not own a house), and engage in religious and cultural activities that marked their identity without fear of persecution. Lisbon's history often gets whitewashed, and many attempts to tell it from diverse perspectives are often delayed or dismissed as not critical. Projects like Goethe Institut's **ReMapping Memories** (re-mapping.eu) is building a more accurate portrayal of Lisbon, but physical evidence of Mocambo's existence is nowhere to be found.

gate at Rua do Borja opens at the same time but closes 15 minutes earlier.

The large lawn near the old greenhouse is ideal for family picnics. When it comes to maintenance, though, this urban park on the north side of Alcântara needs a little love. An improvement project funded by the tourist tax is underway and should be completed by 2027. In the meantime, mind the uneven pavements, loose cobblestones and rogue tree roots poking out of the dirt paths.

Shop & Sightsee at LX Factory
SHOPPING CENTRE

MAP: **14** P126 **B5**

At a former fabric and thread factory, **LX Factory** (lxfactory.com; free) is a must-see on the west side of the neighbourhood. Mind the uneven cobblestones and the occasional traffic as you stroll through the complex browsing alternative shops and admiring street art on industrial-looking, slightly run-

down buildings housing restaurants, cafes, tattoo parlours, art stores and galleries, and one of the world's most beautiful bookshops. With the ever-present bridge over your head, rush hours are always noisier because of the trains and the heavy traffic above, but it just takes a few minutes to get used to.

Get a View of Lisbon from Pilar 7
VIEWPOINT

MAP: **15** P126 **B6**

Ponte 25 de Abril marks the landscape of industrial Alcântara. While engineering enthusiasts will appreciate the interactive exhibition on the history of the bridge at **Experiência Pilar 7** (adult/child €5/free), most rush through it on their way to the top to view Lisbon's industrial quarter, the river and Belém. Although completely safe, the small glass-encased platform and the proximity to the bridge's rushing traffic might feel overwhelming for some.

 ALMADA NEGREIROS' MURALS

In the 1940s, the government commissioned modernist artist Almada Negreiros to create 14 murals for the newly opened boat stations in Alcântara, Gare Marítima de Alcântara and Gare Marítima da Rocha do Conde de Óbidos. The brief was to portray Portugal's greatness, but Negreiros chose the route of artistic independence and painted the country as it was then (backwards, melancholic, poor). The government tried to cover up the murals, which were deemed shameful and inaccurate. After a year-long restoration, visitors can see the murals again (for free). An interpretation centre about the pieces is set to open in 2025.

Best Places for...

See p126 for map of locations

G Budget   **GG** Midrange   **GGG** Top End

Eating

Mediterranean & Portuguese

Último Porto **G**
16 F5

Hidden away at the docks, Último Porto is a well-kept local secret. It serves simple grilled fish paired with top Portuguese wines. *instagram.com/ultimoportorestaurante; noon-4pm Mon-Sat*

Varina da Madragoa **G**
17 H3

A neighbourhood institution, this traditional restaurant offers hearty Portuguese dishes in generous portions. *12.30-3pm & 8-10.30pm Tue-Sun*

Therapist **G**
18 B5

Sustainable and eco-friendly vegan and vegetarian Mediterranean-style cuisine restaurant at LX Factory with lots of gluten-free options. *thetherapist.pt; 9am-7pm Wed-Mon*

Breakfast & Brunch

Mila **G**
19 G4

All-day brunch cafe in Santos that started as a neighbourhood organic grocery store. *milalisbon.com; 9am-5pm*

Fauna & Flora **G**
20 H3

This health-conscious Santos cafe is a standby for affordable light meals and brunch. *faunaflora lisboa.com; 9am-6pm*

Drinking

Wine

Comida Independente
21 H3

No-reservations bar in Santos with wine by the glass, highlighting Portuguese and small-scale makers. Hosts occasional tastings. *comidaindependente.pt; 4-11pm Tue-Fri, noon-11pm Sat*

Shopping

Books & Souvenirs

Salted Books
22 H3

Independent bookshop with English-language books, hosting book-related events. *saltedbooks.com; 10am-6.30pm Tue-Sat, 9am-5pm Sun*

Corredor
23 B5

Local artists' work and original souvenirs sold in the corridor between two warehouses. *instagram.com/corredor_lxfactory; noon-7pm*

Fashion

LX Market
24 A5

Every Sunday, this artisan and vintage market takes over the back lot of LX Factory. *lxmarket.pt; 10am-7pm Sun*

Reuse
25 H3

Popular spot for vintage clothes and accessories. *10.30am-7.30pm*

Sintra

Extravagant romantic palaces and an old Moorish castle make Sintra a top day trip from Lisbon. The unpredictable and often misty weather that peppers the evergreen mountains has inspired artists and local lore for centuries, and the historic centre, a UNESCO World Heritage Site, is suitably picturesque.

PLANNING TIP
Plan for an early start and take a morning train from Rossio. When returning, take any train from Sintra to Lisbon (Entrecampos, Oriente or Rossio), to avoid rush-hour crowds.

Scan this QR code to book tickets for Palácio Nacional da Pena.

Romantic Gardens

Commissioned by local millionaire Carvalho Monteiro, 19th-century **Quinta da Regaleira** *(regaleira.pt; adult/child €12/7)* is an iconic Romantic site that has stirred myths around the estate owner's esoteric habits.

While everyone is turning right to visit **Poço Iniciático** (Initiation Well), turn left to the chapel and the palace instead. Because most visitors wait at the well or skip the palace altogether, you might feel like you have the house to yourself. Sensor lights turn on to lead the way, and information boards in English provide context. Although you can't enter the rooms, there's enough space to see every intricate detail. Architect and set designer Luigi Manini knew how to impress.

There's always a queue to descend into Poço Iniciático. Once you get there, expect to wait in line for at least 30 minutes.

House of Witches

Previously abandoned for years, **Palácio Biester** *(biester.pt; adult/child €12/7)* opened for the first time in 2022 after a beautiful restoration. It's often overlooked by visitors rushing past on their way to neighbouring Regaleira, and it's a shame that this palace known as the House of Witches gets a fraction of the attention.

FRANCISCOMARQUES/SHUTTERSTOCK ©

Manini also designed Palácio Biester, as well as
Villa Sassetti *(parquesdesintra.pt)*, in the middle of
the walking path connecting Sintra's historic centre
to Palácio da Pena and Castelo dos Mouros. This is
a lovely way to reach the uphill monuments and see
the house (from the outside) and the gardens.

Palace & Castle

Book a 3pm ticket for **Palácio Nacional da Pena**
(parquesdesintra.pt; adult/child €20/18) and walk
uphill or catch bus 434 *(scotturb.com; €13.50)*.
Rising from a thickly wooded peak and often
shrouded in swirling mist, this romantic palace is
Sintra's crown jewel. Expect to spend a couple of
hours admiring the gardens, the colourful architecture and each room's intriguing details.

The 10th-century **Castelo dos Mouros** *(parques
desintra.pt; adult/child €12/10)* might be less vis-
ually appealing than its next-door neighbour, but
don't underestimate it. Explore the walls, see the
views and imagine what medieval life was like.

QUICK BREAK
Stop at **Casa
Piriquita** for
an original
travesseiro.
The bakery
has made this
pillow-shaped
puff pastry with
egg cream and
almond filling
since 1862.

Lisbon Toolkit

Alfama (p66)
KERRY MURRAY/LONELY PLANET ©

Family Travel

Lisbon is a family-friendly city with lots of activities for kids of all ages. The city has plenty of public gardens, squares, playgrounds and urban parks where children can unwind and families can stop for a picnic.

Navigating the City

Pushing a pram around town is exhausting (and sometimes dangerous) as you'll have to account for slippery and uneven cobblestones, narrow pavements, badly parked cars and rental e-scooters ditched wherever they ran out of battery. Pack a baby carrier, sling or backpack for a more comfortable experience.

Eating Out

Many restaurants have kids' menus *(menu infantil)* that often feature chips and burger combos, ham and cheese pizzas, pasta with tomato sauce, fish sticks and chicken nuggets. Restaurants without these options usually accommodate requests to whip up a simple omelette or bring an extra side of chips. Highchairs are available for free, but smaller restaurants might have only one.

BREASTFEEDING IN PUBLIC

Breastfeeding in public is legal, but some frown on this behaviour. The airport and some shopping centres have dedicated areas for breastfeeding.

Admission Fees

Top attractions offer free entry for children under 12 and charge half price for older kids. Some have special family tickets.

Public Transport

Kids under three travel for free. They don't need a ticket, but parents might be asked to show the child's ID.

Nappy-changing Facilities

Shopping centres, museums and some attractions, as well as most cafes and restaurants, have nappy-changing facilities. Some are in a separate bathroom specifically for children, but most are inside the women's restrooms or the accessible toilets.

WIKTORY/SHUTTERSTOCK ©

Accommodation

In a city with more hotels than permanent homes, it's easy to find accommodation that fits your travel style and budget.

Where to stay if you love...

Bar-hopping & Clubbing

Bairro Alto (p34) Cheap bars, eclectic cultural hubs and tiny clubs. Noisy by night, the neighbourhood is dead quiet during the day. Has a mix of short-stay apartments and high-end hotels.

HOW MUCH FOR A NIGHT IN

Hostel dorm bed
from €20

Midrange hotel
from €60

High-end hotel in the historic centre
from €150

Indie Cinema & Art Museums

Saldanha (p110) Home to some of the best art collections in the city and an independent cinema that's become a Lisbon institution. Most hotels are midrange or business and close to the metro.

OUR PICK

★

We love to stay in...

Baixa (p52) Long known as the hotel quarter, this popular downtown area has the most accommodation options and is near restaurants, shops, cafes and public transit. It's touristy by day but quiets down after dinner. Lodging is diverse and fits any budget, from hostels and apartment rentals to heritage and midrange chain hotels.

History & Heritage

Graça (p66) Less crowded than the rest of the historic centre. Though not as charming as Alfama, accommodation in Graça is primarily guesthouses and hostels and is more affordable.

High-end Shops & Restaurants

Marquês de Pombal (p110) This area has the highest concentration of designer shops, expensive cafes and fine-dining restaurants. Accommodation ranges from high-end and design hotels to boutique guesthouses.

Architecture & Quiet

Parque das Nações (p96) Ideal for families and fans of contemporary architecture, this neighbourhood is near the metro, buses, urban trains and the airport. Accommodation is primarily international chain hotels.

Food, Drink & Nightlife

Allergies & Intolerances

By law, restaurants and cafes must list ingredients that could trigger an allergic reaction. Most of the time, these ingredients are on the menu, but always inform your server of your allergies before ordering.

HOW TO SAY

I'm allergic to... Faço alergia a...
nuts frutos secos
peanut amendoim
shellfish marisco
dairy products lacticínios
gluten gluten

?

HOW TO ASK...

Is this gluten-free?
Isto é sem gluten?
Does this contain nuts?
Isto contém frutos secos?
Is there a vegan option?
Há alguma alternativa vegan?

── **TOURIST TRAP TASCAS** ──

'Authentic' restaurants and *tascas* (taverns) with menus full of must-try local dishes can be found in the most touristy streets in the Baixa neighbourhood. Avoid places where waiters stand outside to lure you in with special discounts while waving laminated menus with stock photos of the daily specials, sometimes including non-local dishes like Spanish paella.

Starters

In traditional restaurants, waiters bring bread, cheese and olives before you order. These starters aren't complimentary. Check the menu or ask how much it costs, and if it doesn't fit your budget or you simply don't want to eat it, send it back; otherwise, it will be on the bill.

HOW TO... Pay the Bill

Unless the restaurant is busy and needs your table, servers bring the bill only if you ask. Just raise your hand and say, '*A conta, por favor.*'

Splitting the bill: To ask whether you want to split the bill, waiters ask, '*Junto ou separado?*' (together or separate).

Tipping: Tipping isn't mandatory, but some restaurants add a suggested amount to the bill. For card payments, double check how much you're being charged beforehand. For exceptional service, 5% to 10% is standard. For cafes and bars, rounding to the nearest euro. When paying in cash, say, '*fique com o troco*' (keep the change).

PRICE RANGES

The following price ranges refer to the average cost of a main course.

€ less than €15
€€ €15–30
€€€ more than €30

OPENING HOURS

Cafes 7am to 11pm
Restaurants noon to 10pm; some restaurants close after lunch at 3pm and reopen for dinner at 7pm
Snack bars 9am to 10pm

Going Out

Club scene Trendy Lux-Frágil (p81), eclectic Musicbox (p44) and LGBTIQ+ haven Trumps (p50) are cornerstones of Lisbon's clubbing experience.

When to go Head to bars after 11pm and nightclubs after 2am.

At the door Most bouncers refuse entry to visibly intoxicated people. As for why others are turned away, it might depend on the mood of who's working the door, what you wear or the size of the crowd inside. There's no point in arguing or trying to figure it out. Don't take the rejection personally and find the next best place.

Bairro Alto vs Cais do Sodré Bars in Bairro Alto are more casual and usually more affordable, but they aren't allowed to stay open after 2am by law. After Bairro Alto's bars close, continue a night out downhill in Cais do Sodré, where bars close later. Cais do Sodré also has an eclectic selection of clubs that close at 6am.

HOW MUCH FOR A

Pastel de nata from €1.50

Bica (espresso) €0.90–1.50

Glass of wine from €3

Imperial (draught beer) €2–2.50

Shot of *ginjinha* (cherry liqueur) from €1.50

Dinner at a *tasca* €15–20

Small cup of artisanal ice cream €4

Tasting menu at a Michelin restaurant from €190

TOOLKIT FOOD, DRINK & NIGHTLIFE

145

LGBTIQ+ Travellers

Despite historic achievements for LGBTIQ+ rights, not all of Portugal has embraced progress, but Lisbon is fairly open-minded.

LGBTIQ+ Neighbourhoods

All neighbourhoods in Lisbon are welcoming, but some feel safer.

Príncipe Real was a safe space for the community when coming out was 'immoral' and illegal before democracy. It still has one of the highest concentrations of LGBTIQ+-friendly bars and clubs in Lisbon.

In Bairro Alto, you don't need to go to LGBTIQ+-friendly bars to feel free and have a good time. A lot of today's accepting atmosphere in the neighbourhood comes from the legacy of 1980s Frágil, a now-closed bar where everyone was allowed and encouraged to be themselves.

In the historic centre, Graça has welcomed several LGBTIQ+ artistic businesses in the last decade, which seem to be more open to the whole spectrum within the queer community and less worried about strict labels.

OUR PICKS

LGBTIQ+ Clubs

Trumps (p50) For younger clubbers and open to all colours of the rainbow flag.
Finalmente (p50) Lisbon's first gay nightclub has attracted crowds to its nightly drag shows since 1976.
Drama Bar (p81) Take a hint from the name; everything is over the top here, but it's more fun than drama.

ARRAIAL LISBOA PRIDE

In late June, Praça do Comércio fills up with revellers, music, handicrafts, art fairs and street-food stalls for the annual Arraial Lisboa Pride.

NITO/SHUTTERSTOCK ©

QUEER LISBOA

In late September, Cinema São Jorge welcomes Lisbon's week-long International Queer Film Festival. Independent filmmakers and artists compete for several awards.

Resources

● ilga-portugal.pt The country's main LGBTIQ+ organisation. ● variacoes.pt Portuguese LGBTIQ+ Chamber of Commerce and Tourism that lists local companies catering to the community. ● proudlyportugal.pt Travel tips for Lisbon and beyond. ● amplos.pt Nonprofit association of parents of members of the LGBTIQ+ community.

Health & Safe Travel

Lisbon is one of the safest cities in the world but has its fair share of pickpockets and petty thieves.

EARTHQUAKES & TSUNAMIS

Seismic activity in Lisbon is low, but in 2024, the city implemented an evacuation plan in case of an earthquake-caused tsunami. By the river, several signs mark Tsunami Hazard Zones and evacuation routes. If a tsunami is predicted, a loud siren sounds over the city.

Buying Medication

At a *farmácia* (pharmacy), you can buy prescription and nonprescription medication and ask for treatment advice (note that it doesn't replace medical care). A *parafarmácia* (parapharmacy) sells over-the-counter meds only, and the staff isn't qualified to answer health-related concerns. Pharmacies are identified with a green cross and regulated by the government. A *drogaria* (drugstore) sells cosmetics, toiletries and a plethora of other products. However, these shops are not allowed to sell medication, not even over-the-counter tablets.

Alcohol
Fines for drunk driving (having higher than a 0.5 g/L alcohol level) range from €250 to €2500.

QUICK INFO

Fake Charities
Don't donate to volunteers who seem only to approach tourists.

Marijuana
Possessing under 25g of cannabis for personal use and smoking outside isn't illegal.

Public Transport
Always validate your ticket to avoid hefty fines.

Health Care

Seeking attention for medical emergencies at public hospitals is free, whether or not you have insurance. At private hospitals, fees apply and vary according to the health system or insurance you have at home. Most doctors and nurses speak English, though not always perfectly; you're most likely to find fluent English-speaking personnel at private hospitals.

PICKPOCKETING

Often a family business, pickpockets have worked the streets of Lisbon for years. They blend in, disguised as tourists, and cover their hands with scarves or large maps.

Responsible Travel

Follow these tips to leave a lighter footprint, support local and have a positive impact on communities.

Zero Waste Lab Portugal

Mouraria-based nonprofit Zero Waste Lab supports local sustainability projects and green companies with the shared goal of reaching carbon neutrality by 2030. Recent projects include developing a system to recycle plastic toys (plasticreplay.pt) and the interactive Mapa Lixo Zero (lisboalixozero.zerowastelab.pt), which maps sustainable and community-based businesses in Lisbon. Reveste Lisboa focuses on alternatives to fast fashion, organising workshops on how to sew and redesign used clothes. A secondhand shop is in the works.

⚠ Plastic Ban

By law, cafes and restaurants are forbidden to use single-use plastics (coffee stirrers, forks, cups). Plastic bags at all shops cost €0.10. In 2024, Lisbon banned single-use plastic cups for drinking outside bars.

OUR PICK ★

Social Shop

Shop for bargains, vintage clothes and used books at **Dona Ajuda** (p121). All items are donated, and profits go to local social projects.

🚌 Prioritise Public Transit

Lisbon has a good and easy-to-navigate public transit network that delivers you to most of the city's top attractions. On weekday peak hours (7am to 9am and 5pm to 7pm), avoid crowded buses and trams for short distances to allow locals to use the services for commuting.

Resources

- **peggada.com** Verifies ecofriendly and sustainable businesses in Portugal.
- **lisboaparapessoas.pt** Donation-based print and online newspaper about sustainability and local life in Lisbon.

RECYCLING

Recycling bins are widely available in the city. Blue is for paper. Plastic and packaging go in the yellow bin, and green is for glass. Smaller red containers (called *pilhão*) are for used batteries.

ZER

To reduce fossil-fuel pollution levels and traffic in congested areas such as Baixa and the historic centre, Lisbon's city council established two Zonas de Emissões Reduzidas (Reduced Emissions Zones). The first zone was created in 2011 and has been adjusted based on the improvement – or not – of air quality. Only vehicles made after 2000 are allowed in Zone 1, which covers Avenida da Liberdade and Baixa. Zone 2, which includes parts of Avenidas Novas and Alcântara, is open to vehicles made after 1996.

SOCIAL IMPACT RESTAURANT
É Um Restaurante (p123) employs people who are unhoused or have been in the past. **CRESCER** *(crescer. org/en)* is the social organisation behind the restaurant.

Climate Change & Travel

It's impossible to ignore the impact we have when travelling; Lonely Planet urges all travellers to engage with their travel carbon footprint, which will mainly come from air travel. While there often isn't an alternative, travellers can look to minimise the number of flights they take, opt for newer aircrafts and use cleaner ground transport, such as trains. One proposed solution—purchasing carbon offsets—unfortunately does not cancel out the impact of individual flights. While most destinations will depend on air travel for the foreseeable future, for now, pursuing ground-based travel where possible is the best course of action.

The **UN Carbon Offset Calculator** shows how flying impacts a household's emissions

The **ICAO's carbon emissions calculator** allows visitors to analyse the CO_2 generated by point-to-point journeys

Accessible Travel

Public Transport

Historic trams are too narrow to accommodate wheelchair users, and people with reduced mobility might find it hard to get on and off because of the high steps. All Lisbon Metro stations have lifts, but they're often 'temporarily' out of order. Check the Metropolitano de Lisboa website (metrolisboa.pt/en) for status updates on the lifts in real-time.

City Obstacles

People with reduced mobility or visual impairments face some challenges in Lisbon, from uneven, sometimes slippery cobblestones and narrow, partially collapsed pavements to poorly parked cars that force people to go on the road to walk around.

OUR PICK ★

Despite being in an old repurposed church, **Museu do Dinheiro** (p60) provides visitors with disabilities with the best experience. Wheelchair users can access the museum via a low-incline ramp, and lifts access the different floors. People with vision impairments or low vision have access to several tactile replicas and models. All interactive displays are in Portuguese and English. Pre-booked guided tours in sign language are available only in Portuguese (LGP, Língua Gestual Portuguesa), but all informational materials are translated into English.

ACCOMMODATION

Larger and chain hotels usually have rooms equipped for people with disabilities. In hostels, small guesthouses and short-stay apartments (especially in older buildings in the historic centre), it's more difficult to find accessible accommodation.

Travelling Alone

Lisbon is a safe city for solo travellers. Avoid business-centric neighbourhoods, such as Marquês de Pombal, Saldanha and Rato, after office hours on weekdays. They empty out, which could cause a sense of insecurity.

— ATMS & CARD PAYMENTS —

Not all street ATMs are easy to reach for wheelchair users. Some large chain supermarkets and shops have cordless payment machines or place them at a lower level for easier reach.

Resources

● tur4all.com The website of this nonprofit organisation lists accessible attractions, hotels and restaurants based on independent on-site visits.

◯ Nuts & Bolts

◷ Opening Hours

Opening hours may vary based on season. It's common for family-owned cafes and restaurants to close in August for summer holidays and for a couple of weeks after New Year's.

Banks 8.30am–3pm Monday–Friday

Bars 5pm–2am

Cafes 7am–11pm

Post Offices 9am–6pm Monday–Friday. Smaller branches might close for lunch from 1pm to 2pm.

Restaurants noon–10pm

Shops 10am–6pm Monday–Friday; some to 1pm Saturday

Supermarkets 9am–9pm

QUICK INFO

Time zone Western European Time (GMT/UTC)
Country code +351
Emergency number 112
Population 505,000

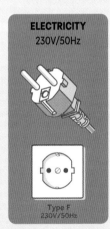

ELECTRICITY
230V/50Hz

Type F
230V/50Hz

🚭 Smoking

Smoking (including e-cigarettes) isn't allowed inside or outside of public buildings, hospitals and schools, inside public transportation, and inside metro stations. It's also prohibited in bars, restaurants, cafes (including outdoor terraces and interior courtyards if they are semi-closed) and hotels unless there's a separate and enclosed area for smokers.

Public Holidays

Shops, banks and post offices are closed on the following *feriados*.

Dia de Ano Novo (New Year's Day) 1 January

Páscoa (Easter) March/April; Good Friday and Easter Sunday

Dia da Liberdade (Liberty Day) 25 April

Dia do Trabalhador (Labour Day) 1 May

Dia de Portugal (Portugal Day) 10 June

Assunção (Assumption) 15 August

Implantação da República (Republic Day) 5 October

Dia de Todos os Santos (All Saints' Day) 1 November

Restauração da Independência (Independence Day) 1 December

Imaculada Conceição (Immaculate Conception) 8 December

Dia de Natal (Christmas Day) 25 December

Language

Portuguese Basics

Hello.
Olá. o·*laa*

Goodbye.
Adeus. a·*de*·oosh

Yes.
Sim. seeng

No.
Não. nawng

Please.
Por favor. poor fa·*vor*

Thank you.
Obrigado/a.
o·bree·*gaa*·doo/da

You're welcome.
De nada. de *naa*·da

Excuse me! (to get attention)
Faz favor! faash fa·*vor*

Excuse me. (to get past)
Com licença. kong lee·*seng*·sa

Sorry.
Desculpe. desh·*kool*·pe

Fast Phrases

Do you speak English?
Fala inglês? *faa*·la eeng·*glesh*

I don't understand.
Não entendo. nowng eng·*teng*·doo

I'd like...   Queria... ke·*ree*·a

a beer.   uma cerveja. *oo*·ma ser·*ve*·zha

a coffee.   um café. oong ka·*fe*

a red/white wine.   um copo de vinho tinto/
                        branco. oong *ko*·poo dc
                        vee·nyoo teeng·too/*brang*·koo

Please bring the bill.
Pode-me trazer a conta. *po*·de·me tra·*zer* a *kong*·ta

How much is it? Quanto custa? *kwang*·too *koosh*·ta

Where can I find the toilets?
Onde são as casas de banho? *ong*·de sowng ash
kaa·zash de *ba*·nyoo

Could you please speak more slowly?
Podia falar mais devagar, por favor? poo·*dee*·a
fa·*laar* maish de·va·*gaar* poor fa·*vor*

Where's an ATM?
Onde há um caixa automático? ong·de aa oong
kai·sha ow·too·*maa*·tee·koo

I'd like a receipt, please.
Queria um recibo, por favor. ke·*ree*·a oong rre·*see*·-
boo poor fa·*vor*

Numbers

 um oong

 dois doysh

 três tresh

 quatro *kwaa*·troo

 cinco *seeng*·koo

⚠ Emergencies

Help! Socorro! *soo·ko·rroo*

Go away! Vá-se embora! *vaa·se eng·bo·ra*

Call ...! Chame ...!   *shaa·me ...*
  a doctor um médico *oong me·dee·koo*
  the police a polícia *a poo·lee·sya*

FALSE FRIENDS

Warning: many Portuguese words look like English words but have a different meaning altogether, eg **salsa** *saal·sa* is 'parsley', not 'sauce' (which is **molho** *mo·lyoo* in Portuguese).

Signs

Saída Exit

Entrada Entrance

Aberto Open

Fechado Closed

Mulheres Women

Homens Men

Casa de Banho Toilets/WC

Informação Information

(Não) Há Vaga (No) Vacancy

Não Fumar No Smoking

Não Fotografar No Photography

Proibido Prohibited

🎧 Listen for

Passaporte paa·sa·*por*·te **Passport**
Visto *veesh*·too **Visa**
Posso ajudar? *po*·soo a·zhoo·*daar* **Can I help you?**
O que deseja? oo ke de·*ze*·zha **What would you like?**

——— SLANG TO LISTEN OUT FOR ———

então A flexible word that changes meaning at each inflection. It can be a short form of a concerned question or a replacement for 'hello' *(então?)*, a polite 'watch it' *(então!)*, or a pause someone makes before starting a lengthy explanation *(então...)*

t'fona-me A super-contracted short form for *telefoname* (call me)

pá Translates as bread; however, is usually used as an interjection meaning 'man!' or 'dude!'. Depending on context, *pá* is also used in the place of 'uhh...' when you are thinking.

tipo Used in the same context as how many English speakers use 'like'; however, it literally translates as 'type'

 6
seis saysh

 7
sete *se*·te

 8
oito *oy*·too

 9
nove *no*·ve

 10
dez desh

Index

Sights p000   Map pages p000

See also separate subindexes for:
- Eating p156
- Drinking p157
- Shopping p158

Eating

🍷 **Drinking**

Send Us Your Feedback

We love to hear from travellers – your comments help make our books better. We read every word, and we guarantee that your feedback goes straight to the authors. Visit lonelyplanet.com/contact to submit your updates and suggestions.

Note: We may edit, reproduce and incorporate your comments in Lonely Planet products such as guidebooks, websites and digital products, so let us know if you are happy to have your name acknowledged. For a copy of our privacy policy visit lonelyplanet.com/legal.

Acknowledgements

Cover photograph: Principe Real, Lisbon. Hemis / AWL Images ©

Back photograph: Castelo dos Mouros, Sintra. saiko3p/Shutterstock ©

THIS BOOK

Destination Editor
Annemarie McCarthy

Cartographer
Anita Banh

Production Editor
Kate James

Book Designer
Norma Brewer

Assisting Editors
Felicity Hughes, Lauren Keith, Amy Lysen, Charlotte Orr, Fionnuala Twomey

Cover Researcher
Gwen Cotter

Thanks to
Imogen Bannister, Saralinda Turner

Although the authors and Lonely Planet have taken all reasonable care in preparing this book, we make no warranty about the accuracy or completeness of its content and, to the maximum extent permitted, disclaim all liability arising from its use.

Published by Lonely Planet Global Limited

CRN 554153

7th edition – Mar 2025

ISBN 978 1 83758 355 3

© Lonely Planet 2025

Photographs © as indicated 2025

10 9 8 7 6 5 4 3 2 1

Printed in China